SALT, LIGHT, & KIDS

Parenting Well in Today's Culture

STEVE HINES

Chris,
I pray blessings on you and your
wife my friend. I also pray your
influence for good is ever-increasing.
We need to have lunch soon!

1 Cor. 4: 3-4

Steve Hines

X

BATTLEGROUND
PRESS

NASHVILLE, TN

X

BATTLEGROUND
PRESS

Cover and Interior Design: Sarah Siegand

Editor: Ashley Hagan

ISBN: 9798218160494 (paperback)

ISBN: 9798218160500 (ebook)

*This book is dedicated to my wife Leigh Ann,
the most amazing mother and the most
wonderful human being I've ever met.*

TABLE OF CONTENTS

FOREWORD

BY CHRIS HODGES

If I know anything about good parenting, it's that it requires being intentional. Parenting is not an exact science, and ultimately all you can do is your best. But doing your best intentionally and consistently almost always makes a profound positive difference in the lives of your children.

Tammy and I, like most parents, learned as we went along, discovering that what worked well for one child did not always work for another. Our parenting journey wasn't perfect, but all of our kids—now adults—love us, love God, and love the Church and for that we're so thankful. How did we do it? We tried to stay authentic, fun, full of grace, and we never let up—I mean never. We worked on our relationship with our kids every day, intentionally engaging and encouraging and equipping each child as best we could. The only time we had problems is when

I was absent—too busy with the church or distracted by other demands.

Tammy and I also questioned friends and families we knew and admired for their parenting style. We prayed daily, sometimes hourly, for wisdom, patience, and the strength to show our children the same unconditional love our Heavenly Father shows us, asking Him to bless and protect each of our kids. Of course, we also read what the Bible said about parenting along with lots of books by experts. While there was an abundance of parenting books, we found only a few that were based on God's Word and tested by authentic experience.

Which is why I am so excited about my friend Steve Hines' new book, *Salt, Light, & Kids*. It's a call to parents to raise their kids up as salt and light based on Matthew 5, leading and serving by example while shepherding the precious gift of each son or daughter. This book both challenges and encourages, reminding all moms and dads that the choices they make today will affect their children for the rest of their lives.

Filled with Scripture applied accurately and practically, *Salt, Light, & Kids* provides insight on how to avoid the traps of the enemy in today's often overwhelming social media-driven culture. The wisdom Steve offers has been tested by his own experience as well as interactions with dozens of other parents. His humble approach never presumes he and his wife, Leigh Ann, are perfect parents—only that they want to generously offer what they wished they had known starting out.

While Steve and Leigh Ann may not have been perfect, they provided a model of parenting and marriage that inspired so many of us, Tammy and I included. They have been dear friends to us since the beginning of Church of the Highlands (the church I founded in 2001 in Birmingham, AL). While they now live in Nashville, their participation and contribution was instrumental in the formation of Highlands. Back when we were meeting at Mountain Brook High School, Steve sang on the worship team, and he and Leigh Ann led numerous small groups, and strongly supported our church financially when we really needed it the most. He's not only a good husband and incredible father, but Steve is also just a fun guy to be around.

You don't need to take my word for it, though. Whether you're expecting your first child or in the frontlines of the teen years, you will discover *Salt, Light, & Kids* to be an invaluable resource for your parenting journey. With Steve as your guide and God's Word as your lamp, you will return to this book again and again. I know you will not only be blessed by what you're about to read, but you will also be inspired to be the best parent possible.

CHRIS HODGES
Senior Pastor, Church of the Highlands
Birmingham, Alabama
Author of *Out of the Cave* and *Pray First*

INTRODUCTION

WHY THIS BOOK?

I had never planned or even thought about writing a book on parenting. Wasn't on my radar, wasn't on my mind, wasn't something I'd even considered. Then one day in the fall of 2022, I was sitting in a car in the quiet, watching my one-year-old granddaughter Sage sleep in her car seat. Out of the blue, like a bolt of lightning, God clearly said I was to write a book on parenting. It was probably the strongest I've ever been prompted in a single moment by Him about anything, and in an instant I knew what my next immediate step in life was to be. I wasn't sure why, but for some reason I was to write this book.

It's been exciting to watch the direction and thoughts contained in the book change and evolve as I wrote and as He prompted. It has felt good, feeling at times like I was just a scribe, writing down what I was told.

So, here goes. In this book you will read about some

of the things our four-person family has experienced, some of the situations we've encountered, and some of the principles about parenting well that I and my wife Leigh Ann have learned through trial, through error, and through reward.

May God bless you and make your heart a receiving vessel as you read these pages.

CHAPTER ONE

PARENTING WELL

Three decades. It's hard to believe I have been a parent for that long. And what a time warp it has been because it really does seem like it has all passed by in the blink of an eye. Over the last thirty years, parenting has given me many of my greatest joys, and looking back, I can honestly say I really do appreciate every moment. I love my wife more than ever, and my kids are two of my best friends in the entire world. But getting to this point has not been a road that was without challenge.

Parenting is hard. Let me rephrase that—parenting WELL is hard. And it doesn't help that the culture today presents more obstacles than ever to our children being able to become selfless, well-rounded, responsible, and good human beings—salt-of-the-earth people, as the saying goes.

If you've ever heard someone called "salt-of-the-earth,"

then you can bet that person is a good, solid, decent, hard-working person. In the Bible in Matthew 5:13, Jesus also says, "You are the salt of the earth…" and was speaking to his followers at that time. He was encouraging them to have the flavor of God, or His influence and attributes, such as love, patience, grace, and forgiveness, and for these qualities to be evident for everyone to see. In both the earthly and the Biblical sense, these are all qualities that I'm sure we desire for our children and for ourselves. In that same chapter, in verse 14, Jesus says, "You are the light of the world…." Being a light in this context means letting love, grace, and compassion shine through us into what can be a pretty dark world, just like Jesus did.

In the world in which our children are growing up, they hear so many voices and have so many outside influences that it's almost not fair to them. With all these influences being magnified by technology and social media, our parenting becomes even more of a challenge. Helping our kids become true salt-of-the-earth people might seem more difficult with each passing day. There are so many opinions being expressed through the media, blogs, podcasts, and social media, and it seems like every human on earth has a platform to add their ideas to the mix. Unfortunately, this relatively new phenomenon has created the perfect recipe for confusion. The good news is that if you are willing to minimize other people's and even your own opinions and filter everything through what God's Word says, parenting decisions will suddenly become much more clear. Right now, perhaps more than ever, there's a battle for the hearts and minds of children going on between culture and parents. And parents, it's a battle that can be won!

If we want to win the battle as parents, we need to have the desire to truly parent well. If we want to parent well, we must resolve to make parenting more important than almost anything else and give it the effort and attention that's required. Choosing the path of least resistance in parenting is rarely the right choice, and to consistently put it at the high level of priority it deserves might at times be an inconvenience. As a reward for this effort, the relationship between you and your children can and should become very meaningful, very unique, and very special. Parenting can lead to some of the most satisfying times in life, and the relationships you build with your children can be so deeply fulfilling that it really can't be put into words. I mean, how cool is it that people you made can turn out to be some of your deepest and most gratifying relationships?

It can also lead to times where you really don't know which way to turn or what to do, and you might find yourself in a whirlwind of uncertainty and doubt. Should I punish them or let it slide? Should I let my daughter have a boyfriend at age fifteen? Should I cut something out of the kids' schedule so we don't feel frantic all the time? Should I let my child go to this party where I suspect underage drinking will be happening? Should I confront my child's teacher about a perceived unfair slight? Without a doubt, parenting comes with a lot of uncertainty, and many fellow parents may say yes to things for their own children that you would say no to, which can make it even tougher for you to stick to your convictions.

One day when my son was about eight years old, he suddenly blurted out, "What is sex?" Talk about a shock! After a stunned silence, my wife looked at him and said, "Why do you ask?" He looked back at her and said, "Earlier I was looking at Mamaw's driver's license, and she made an F in it." There followed a big laugh and a big sigh of relief because we weren't quite ready to have that conversation just yet. My young son obviously did not have an understanding of that sensitive subject, and sometimes parents can feel like they have a similar level of understanding when it comes to parenting.

It can be hard to have an objective overview of a particular point in time when you are right in the middle of it, but having been alive for six decades has provided me with a pretty good panoramic view of some of the changes in society over the last few decades. It has also provided me with some perspective of today's culture, and, quite honestly, I have a lot of compassion for parents with children at home or in college. Between their peers, their teachers, their TikTok feeds, their music, the media, and technology, children of today have many competing voices that make it difficult for parents to be the most impactful voice in their lives. But with effort and dedication, you really can be their biggest influence.

I often think about the generations beginning from my parents (who are 93 and 87 years old) down to me, then to my kids and grandkids, and with each generation, society overall has noticeably changed. People's sense of entitlement has steadily grown, and activities and lifestyles that used to be considered wrong are now accepted and even embraced. Sexuality has become one big quagmire of confusion and open experimentation, even at very young ages, and now it almost has a kind of lawlessness to it. Technology has exploded, creating parenting challenges that have never been faced before in history. Life has become busy and complicated. And, right in the middle of all this, most parents still want to parent well.

We are all guaranteed to make mistakes as parents. There is no doubt that my parenting journey was filled with them. But there is a big difference between making a wrong parenting decision, even after much deliberation, and making a wrong decision because you as a parent didn't invest the thought and time to consider the options and make the best decision you could. As life becomes busier and as more and more things compete for our attention, parents must make a conscious decision about where they are going to spend their time and effort. Will peripheral things like golf or talking on the phone or scrolling through social media or even our jobs take too much of our attention, or will the desire to parent well receive the high level of focus it deserves?

I graduated from college with a degree in accounting and had good grades (except for that terrible art appreciation class!). During my last semester I took an accounting class on auditing and made an A. After graduation I left for an accounting/auditing job with a national accounting firm, and I thought I was as prepared as humanly possible to begin my professional career. Little did I know. About one week into my career, I realized I did not know much of anything about real-life accounting, and my new job wasn't at all like that auditing class I had taken a few months before. This was much more difficult, and reading textbooks and doing well on tests in college did not equate to success with my real-life job. It was an eye-opener once I found myself having to go to actual clients, being asked real questions, and having to make real decisions that affected real people.

Interestingly, I had the same thing occur when we had our two kids. Leigh Ann and I have a married daughter named Madeline with two daughters of her own, and a married son named Max. Before Madeline was born, Leigh Ann checked out a couple of parenting books at the library, we both went to two out of six Lamaze birthing classes, and then we sailed into parenthood confidently and erroneously thinking, "We know how to handle this." Shortly after becoming parents, it became evident that we had no idea what we were doing. Who was this little ball of humanity? Do we let her cry at night? Why won't she eat? Why does Madeline have the curse of all baby curses—colic? And of course, we did not have the Internet to search for answers; we were pretty much just winging it. It wasn't long before a second tiny human followed, and fortunately my son Max was one of the easiest babies that has ever existed on earth (the parenting challenges he would raise were to come later in his life). And all along the way as they grew up and we were trying to figure out this whole parenting thing, we would try to find comfort and solace in the fact that we were trying as hard as we could and doing the best we knew how, even if we weren't sure we were doing it right.

For us, our home was and is based on our Christian faith, and God through His providence and Spirit got us through many of the challenges Leigh Ann and I faced as parents. Whether your family is part of the Christian faith or not, the principles found in the Bible such as humility, serving others, placing others before yourself, working hard, being responsible, being honest, boldly standing up to things you know are not right, and doing everything with excellence still apply. We personally drew upon those Biblical principles as often as possible, and in many ways we looked at our family as being the most important small group we could ever be a part of. We made sure our own four-person family small group came first in our time, energy, and priority.

Looking back, I think all four of us would agree that my kids' growing up years were a lot of fun and very ful-filling, and today we are all very close. But getting through those years had its share of bumps and bruises. If someone comes up now and tells Leigh Ann and me what good people they think our kids are, we thank them, and then under our breath we say, "That's why we are half-dead!" Getting Madeline and Max to the point of being responsible, well-rounded young adults took a great deal of our energy and commitment, but it was a sacrifice we gladly made.

While reflecting over my three decades as a parent, I've come to the strong conclusion that one of the keys to being able to call yourself a successful parent is being able to look back and say, "I may have messed up at times, but I gave it everything I had." Even to this day, with our children as adults, Leigh Ann and I are still—although in different ways—actively parenting, and I bet my mom would say the same thing. I guess it really is true that parenting never stops.

Parents, you obviously care about parenting if you are taking the time to read this book. Wanting to do a great job in parenting is the noblest of desires and efforts, and I applaud you for wanting to do it well. At the outset, there are a few things I'd like you to know.

Parenting well will require thoughtfulness, compassion, and complete dedication.

It will require discernment and wisdom, even when you are in the middle of all the parenting madness.

It will require the humility to know when you are wrong, and then the ability to admit it and make the necessary changes.

It will require keeping a keen eye on how much control the world has on your children and the courage to stand up and say no to the things that are just not good.

It will require not worrying about what other people say or think or believe when it comes to your parenting decisions.

It will require standing firm when your kids beg you to change a decision you've made that you know to be the right decision.

It will require leading by example, because if your children hear one thing from you but see something different, they will not respect your words.

For Leigh Ann and me, it also required a whole lot of prayer for insight as to how to do it best, both in specific situations and in the overall arc of our kids growing up.

Finally, parenting well requires an attitude of "I'm going to leave it all on the field." In sports, leaving it all on the field means giving it everything you have and doing everything you can to help your team. As parents, you don't ever want to let yourself be in a position of looking back and wishing you had done more or tried harder.

All along the way, Leigh Ann and I never thought we had it all figured out, and we definitely made our fair share of parenting mistakes. But I can truly say that we always gave it 100 percent. We weren't concerned when we found ourselves parenting differently than other parents, and we found out that sometimes parenting well actually calls for inaction instead of action. We learned that trying at all costs to keep our kids happy all the time was not parenting well, and sometimes we had to make decisions that our kids were not fans of. We always tried to make decisions that were in the best interests of Madeline and Max, and we never let ourselves fall into the trap of thinking that parenting is a popularity contest.

Be encouraged! With focus and effort, parenting well is achievable, attainable, and amazing. Be confident in that, embrace your role, and give it all you've got!

TO CONSIDER:

1. What does the term "salt-of-the-earth" mean to you?

2. What changes in culture have you seen in your lifetime?

3. Do you think it is important to use the Bible as the main authority when making parenting decisions?

4. What is the difference between parenting and parenting well?

5. What do you hope to gain from this book?

CHAPTER TWO

THE SIMPLE LIFE: HERE'S A STICK AND SOME DIRT

*"Better one handful with tranquility than two
handfuls with toil and chasing after the wind."*
Ecclesiastes 4:6

LET'S GO RETRO

Whether you are an adult or a child, life today is complex. There are distractions that pull at us every second of every day, and there's constant competition for our time and attention. Whether it's technology, media, concerts, sporting events, or just general activities, it seems that everything is bigger, brighter, louder, and more stimulating than it ever has been. At times it almost feels like things have to be over the top to even get a mild level of recognition and response from us. Society seems to have lost the idea that simple can be good.

I was a kid in the 1960s and '70s, and sometimes I long for those days. There were no video games, no Internet, no cell phones, and everything was simple. Life was basically going to school, doing your homework, playing with friends, and going to bed. I vividly remember sitting in my backyard by myself with a stick and drawing racing tracks and making tunnels in the dirt for my Hot Wheels cars, and I had a blast doing it. Most kids today would find that boring, but back then we had to make our own simple fun. We didn't know any better, and life was good.

IT'S OKAY TO NOT BE BUSY

Kids today have so many things to grab their attention and so many things to distract them that I sometimes wonder how they know which way is up or down. By the age of one or two, most kids already have electronic devices in their hands and require constant stimulation to stay happy. A car ride with mom or dad requires a laptop or phone so they can watch a pulsing cartoon or video, and if they're older, so they can text their friends non-stop or be on social media for hours. Talking at meals? Forget it. Texting or looking at Instagram or Snapchat or TikTok is a lot more fun. Many times, I have seen entire families sitting in a restaurant looking intently at their phones for the entire meal, and that screams of sensory overload and missed relationship opportunities.

Striving to have your family's lives have a sense of order and routine will do wonders in creating a happy family dynamic. In 1 Corinthians 14:33, it says, "For God is not a God of disorder but of peace...." While this verse in its Biblical context is talking about worship, I believe it can be applied to our overall daily lives as well.

Filling up every second of every day with activities and entertainment causes even very young children to be bored easily. When the machines and activities and stimulations stop, they don't know what to do. Unfortunately, many parents feed that unhealthy cycle by always making sure their kids are entertained and have something to do, and then something right after that thing, and then something right after that thing...you get the picture. And if there's a minute of downtime, it is panic time.

If you feel that you must keep your kids busy all the time in order to be a good parent, then I encourage you to reconsider. Keeping children's lives relatively simple and structured leads to a less cluttered mind, and I'm convinced that the hyperactivity of schedules and the constant barrage of distractions has played a part in the significant increase in mental health issues in today's children. According to a recent CDC study, persistent feelings of sadness and hopelessness in teenagers increased 44 percent between 2009 and 2019[1], and that was even before the pandemic hit. I believe there are a lot of factors that contributed to that pre-pandemic increase, but it's interesting to note the increase basically mirrors the rise of social media use and advances in technology, which leads to more cluttered minds. Even after these alarming trends, the pandemic happened and was a Mike Tyson gut-punch to our children.

Let me be clear: I'm not saying that children need to sit and stare into space for hours. It is okay for them to have things that occupy their minds and their time a good bit of the day. But kids can become overstimulated if they always have the greatest and most exhilarating toy or game or activity on earth. If those activities take up every single waking moment, that can lead to some big issues for their

---

1   *"Mental Health Among Adolescents." CDC.Gov. Centers for Disease Control and Prevention, January 1, 2021. https://www.cdc.gov/nchhstp/ newsroom/docs/factsheets/dash-mental-health.pdf.*

mental health. Like many things in life, a healthy balance is best.

Most of the time, simple is good, and you as a parent can do a lot to make sure the schedules for your children stay manageable and healthy. This will reduce stress on the kids and on you as parents and cause both of you to appreciate the awesome life moments when they come. It's a challenging tightrope walk, but a very worthy one to attempt.

PARENTS CAN DEFLECT AND LESSEN THE NEED FOR BUSYNESS

My wife Leigh Ann is a great mother and has always loved being a mom. One of the things she did well was how she artfully managed keeping our kids from developing a constant need for Grade A entertainment. When Madeline was younger, Leigh Ann would set her up with craft projects and then let her spend time working at her own pace, helping when necessary. It wasn't boring for Madeline, but it also wasn't a constant ride on Space Mountain. There were lots of times when we all had over-the-top fun, but we always made sure that Madeline spent a good bit of time entertaining herself. Ultimately, that helped her creativity, her independence, and her overall personal development.

Same thing for Max. Early on, we made sure he had many opportunities to figure out how to entertain himself, and it was cool watching him do that over the younger years. He would go into the playroom and build Lincoln Log houses by himself for hours, and he would play with his little plastic army men non-stop (we still have all those little men!). We made sure he learned as a very young child to entertain himself in simple ways, and that has paid off for him in his adult life.

Overall, Leigh Ann and I tried to consistently make sure both Madeline and Max had regular times where they didn't rely on outside activities or people for entertainment. This encouraged them to develop their own creativity and helped their minds to mature and become more independent. It was definitely more challenging to keep life simple when they became teenagers, and at times during those years it felt like a crazy ride that wouldn't ever stop. But when they were young, we made sure they developed the ability to entertain themselves.

TIME MARGINS ARE BENEFICIAL

I've always been an advocate for keeping margins within family and individual schedules. What I mean by that is making sure no one in the family is so consistently booked up that there's no opportunity for down time or room to adjust your schedule for unexpected or more important things that might come along. Keeping margins with time and within your family's schedule is important because always scrambling to get to the next appointment or activity is an unhealthy way to live.

If you consistently feel you're ten minutes behind schedule with your kids, then your schedule is probably too busy. Look for activities that may not be essential and consider getting rid of them. If your son is playing two sports at one time, he may need to play only one. If your daughter is going to dance and then to soccer and then to gymnastics, reconsider if three activities are wise. Being in a rush every second of every day leads to anxiety and stress, both for the kids and for you.

As an example, youth sports are a popular activity for many families, and sports can teach very valuable life lessons. Working hard, learning the team concept, validation of effort, learning how to handle adversity, submitting to authority—all of these are direct life lessons kids can learn through involvement in sports. However, if you as a parent allow youth sports to totally dominate your child's life, leaving no room for anything else, it can lead to burnout and resentment on the part of your child. A lot of boys and girls these days burn out on sports by the time they get to high school because they were consumed by sports in their early years, and this is unfortunate. I spent over a decade coaching boys in junior high and high school and saw this phenomenon firsthand. Kids as young as seven or eight years old play year-round travel ball and tournaments, and this can lead to some of the anxiety and stress we all know exists in many young people. Allowing breaks between sports seasons and not letting your child be at the ball field six or seven days per week for months on end allows some breathing room in your family schedule and will help you have a healthier home and a happier child.

While extra-curricular activities can be stressful and time-consuming, so can achieving in school. Some parents put an almost unbearable pressure on their child to achieve good grades and ACT/SAT scores, and it can ultimately be counterproductive. Don't get me wrong—I believe giving full effort and making the best grades you can is very important. But if your child is feeling constant, overbearing pressure to achieve good grades, and if he or she has the sense of potential doom towards schoolwork, it might be too much pressure. If tutors are being brought in, not for help in a troubled area but to achieve unrealistic academic goals, and if there are weekend cram sessions and all-nighters and constant stress, then it might be a little much.

When I was young, we didn't do any ACT prep work and just showed up one Saturday and took the test, hoping for the best. That probably wasn't the best way to negotiate it, but today I see kids who literally have panic attacks about their ACT or SAT tests and scores. And, along with that comes multiple retaking of the test, numerous tutors, and a huge level of dread and doom. Parents, there is a healthy balance that needs to be struck regarding grades and test scores. Absolutely teach your children the concept of giving their best effort and expect them to do as well as possible. But make sure not to cross the line into overbearing oversight and constant pressure to achieve, because it can backfire on both them and you.

ROUTINES ARE ROUTINELY AWESOME

Keeping a regular family routine simplifies active lives and adds a sense of security. Routines can be a challenge to instill, but they are valuable for the entire family. For instance, we as a family always had dinner together, and those times at the dinner table were some of the best we spent as a family. It wasn't always easy to make it happen, but until my kids left for college, we tried to make sure having dinner together (with no phones present) was a daily occurrence.

I owned a mortgage company when our kids were growing up, and I was busy beyond belief for many years. But if I had to work late, I would try to come home when possible and have dinner with the family and then go back to work once the kids were going to bed. It made for later nights for me, but the family dinner time was just that important. A meal together can be an amazing experience, and in some ways meals can even be considered spiritual experiences. Being together with your entire family for an hour, talking about important or unimportant things, and giving each other undivided attention is awesome. Doing it every day is even more awesome. I encourage you as a parent to guide your family schedule so that you have meals together every day, and those times of breaking bread will create deeper family bonds than almost anything else.

We also implemented a regular sleep schedule with the same routine every night. When they were young, our routine at bedtime included things like reading a book and saying our prayers. and we were consistent with the routine and the time they went to bed. My children appreciated it, as regular routines lead to an overall sense of stability, which is particularly important with younger children. Of course, once they got older, the bedtime became later and the routine disappeared, but even into their teenage years, we did the best we could to make sure they got their sleep because a child (or adult) who is not getting enough sleep is going to find it difficult to lead a productive and fulfilling life.

A valuable part of any family nightly routine is planning for the next day. Talking through what the next day holds and where everybody needs to be at what time is less stressful than just figuring it out in the morning. Doing just a little planning ahead will reduce the chaos and stress and lead to a more simple and happy life for everyone.

CLEANLINESS IS NEXT TO GODLINESS

Another way to simplify your children's lives is to reduce the physical clutter in your home and to have them do the same. If you can't walk across the playroom floor because it's covered in junk, you might want to get rid of some junk. It's probably not a good idea to buy them another toy every time you go to the store or to allow other relatives or people to give them more stuff than they need. Teach them the importance of being organized people, to be aware of the messes, and to pick up after themselves. A clean living area will encourage organization and order, which will bleed over into other areas of their lives. The playroom or their bedroom doesn't have to be as clean as an army barracks, but it should be relatively neat—and your kids should be the ones doing most, or at least a good portion, of the cleaning and organizing. If they get in the habit, I can promise their future spouses will thank you for it!

An even larger issue is the mental clutter our kids experience and feel. The constant use of devices to access social media platforms, apps, and video games can make your child's brain look like that cluttered playroom floor. A phone can easily turn from something useful to something that dominates life, and in odd ways the technology addiction can be just as powerful as a drug addiction. According to the American Academy of Child and Adolescent Psychiatry, preteens average four to six hours and teenagers up to nine hours per day looking at screens.[2] Different studies on this topic vary in small amounts, but if we assume an overall average of seven screen hours per day for kids, that equates to over one hundred 24-hour days used for screen time in one year. That's scary. Not helping is the fact that studies, such as one recently done by the *Journal of Adolescent Health*, attribute these large screen time numbers to other issues, such as an increase in obsessive-compulsive disorder (OCD) behavior[3]. We will talk much more about this subject in chapter eight, but just know that there is probably nothing you can do as a parent that is more effective in keeping your children's lives simple than reasonably limiting their use of technology and their screen time, and then talking to them about the reasons why you are doing the limiting.

---

[2]   *"Screen Time and Children." Aacap.Org. American Academy of Child & Adolescent Psychology, February 1, 2020. www.aacap.org/AACAP/Families_and_Youth/Facts_for_Families/FFF-Guide/Children-And-Watching-TV-054.aspx.*

[3]   *Hou, Chia-Yi. "Screen-time Linked to OCD in Youth: Study." Thehill. Com. The Hill, December 12, 2022. https://thehill.com/changing-america/well-being/mental-health/3769040-screen-time-linked-to-ocd-in-youth-study/.*

To live a simplified life, we as parents must avoid the temptation to make sure our kids have something amazing to do every second of every day and allow them to entertain themselves at times. If children lead a non-chaotic and relatively structured life, they likely will become adults who are independent thinkers with a healthy sense of stability. A constantly overstimulated mind makes the normal times seem boring and the boring times seem like torture. But a mind and body that is not always on full speed ahead is a mind that has room to breathe and think and grow.

TO CONSIDER:

1. Do you feel like your family is constantly overly busy? How does busyness affect your overall family dynamic?

2. Are there any areas that you as a parent put too much pressure on your child?

3. Are there any activities you could and should remove from your own or your children's schedules that would make life better for everyone?

4. Does your family have any regular routines, such as having dinner together?

5. Do you limit the time your children can use technology?

CHAPTER THREE

IT'S YOUR RESPONSIBILITY TO TEACH THEM RESPONSIBILITY

"Whatever your hand finds to do, do it with all of your might..." Ecclesiastes 9:10

PUT 'EM TO WORK

I love when I meet someone I consider to be a responsible person—somebody who will do what they say they're going to do, someone I can count on to finish a job, and someone who does whatever they do with all of their might. It's a quality that is very easy to admire, and it takes great focus on the part of parents to develop a sense of responsibility in their children.

SALT, LIGHT, & KIDS

Starting at about the age of five, our kids were required to have a list of chores to do every Saturday morning. Nothing big or that took all day, but just a few things they had to accomplish before they got to play. We had the same deal with them up until they were grown. Whatever the age, they always had things they were responsible for around the house.

Of course, they didn't like it at first, but they eventually got to the point of waking up on Saturday knowing they had to do their chores, accepting it and no longer complaining about it. We intentionally made the chores a pretty decent list of things, but never enough to make them totally resent the chores (or us). For their efforts, we would reward them with allowance money so they could see the benefit of their labor. Having them feel like servants wasn't our goal, but teaching them responsibility was. We also made sure they understood that they were contributing to our overall family so that their work hopefully produced a sense of inner worth.

As the kids grew older, the chores became more and more detailed. The goal wasn't to make our lives as parents easier; it was to teach the kids some life skills, teach them about responsibility, and teach them about doing things with excellence as the Bible so often talks about. It is easy to have an "I'll do it myself" attitude as parents because we generally can get certain things done much more quickly than if our kids do it or help us do it. But think about the lessons your kids can learn from being involved in completing certain tasks and the time you get to spend together with them that you otherwise would not. It may be more inconvenient for you to involve them, but the benefits for your children far outweigh the inconvenience. As Ann Landers once said, "It is not what you do for your children, but what you have taught them to do for themselves that will make them successful human beings."

THE LONG ROAD TO RESPONSIBILITY

One Saturday when Max was a teenager, Leigh Ann asked him to do some yard work. He was supposed to rake and blow leaves, and it was a pretty big job. After a while, it became obvious to her that he was going to do a halfway job at best and with a bad attitude to boot, something that was common for him at that point in his life. Leigh Ann saw the terrible and incomplete job he had done, so she asked him if he was finished. When he mumbled yes, she asked if he was sure. Once again, he mumbled yes. She didn't get angry. She just said, "Okay," took her leaf blower, and blew all his leaves back where they were before he started. Then she turned around and told him to do it right this time. She wasn't angry or yelling; she was just going to teach him a lesson about doing things right the first time and finishing strong. He sat and stared in stunned silence at first, and then begrudgingly started all over, having wasted two hours of his time by intentionally doing a poor job. From that moment on, he rarely took shortcuts and stopped doing a halfway job with yard work or his other responsibilities at home.

To some it may sound like we were a bit too harsh with Max in that instance, but when Max was in his early twenties, he told me that one of the greatest things we ever did for him was requiring him to do chores and encouraging him to do things with excellence. It taught him a work ethic that he carried into his career and other areas of his life, and he noticed those were things that many of his friends were lacking. That conversation was one of the most validating times I ever experienced as a parent.

During that same time, I had another "stake in the ground" moment with Max. I coached Max for many years during his lacrosse career, and if you know anything about lacrosse, you know that after a practice there will be tons of lacrosse balls that have ended up in the woods from missed shots. We required the players to go around after each practice and look for lost balls. When Max was in ninth grade, he had the "BMOC" (Big Man On Campus) syndrome because he was a talented player who thought he was too good to have to look for balls. I can remember asking (I mean telling) him almost every day to go look for balls, and he would walk as slowly as he possibly could with a frown, maybe picking up one ball. Fast forward to his senior year. I remember a specific day where I noticed that he was the first person to head to the woods after practice to look for balls, and I hadn't said anything to him about going. He was doing it totally on his own, and he did that every day his senior year. I loved the picture that painted of him having matured in humility and responsibility over those four years, and it was at least partially due to the fact that Leigh Ann and I had taken some uncomfortable, and at times inconvenient, stances on things that helped him become a more humble and responsible person.

QUESTIONS, NOT COMMANDS

To develop a sense of responsibility in your children, it is also important to let your child do the thinking about his or her tasks whenever possible instead of you giving orders and then coming behind to make sure everything is done and accounted for. For instance, instead of saying, "Don't forget your homework," you could ask, "Have you got everything?" This accomplishes the goal of reminding them about getting the homework to school but will also cause your children to take personal responsibility for making sure it does. Another option is to not mention it at all and let them suffer the consequences. When parents handle everything their children do or are responsible for, the children's sense of responsibility can be put on autopilot because they know their parents will take care of whatever it is. Including a child in the responsibility of day-to-day things encourages him to grow into a responsible person.

WHAT'S A W-2?

I believe it's important for a teenager to have a real job with an actual employer during the summers of high school and college. Nothing teaches responsibility better than having a job delivering pizza or bagging groceries or working at a daycare changing diapers, and the employer/employee dynamic is not something your child should experience for the first time heading into full-time employment after high school or college. Your children may give you every reason they shouldn't have to work, but a person who doesn't know what it's like to have a boss is walking into a potential disaster when starting a career.

Madeline has always been a hard worker, and that's something we've always been proud of and grateful for. Through the years, she's had various jobs such as babysitting, working as a nanny, working at a local boutique, and working at a high-end jeweler. She didn't always love her jobs, but having those jobs helped teach her people skills, how to work hard, and the rewards of a paycheck. Fortunately, she had a great work ethic from early on and was successful at all the jobs she held prior to being an adult. Leigh Ann and I were grateful that God instilled that in her, and employers have always responded positively to her. It's kind of crazy, but to this day she gets offered jobs almost everywhere she goes, and we smile every time that happens.

Max also worked in high school at lacrosse camps, stringing lacrosse sticks, and providing one-on-one lessons. His first "real" job experience happened one summer after his sophomore year at Belmont University. He asked if he could stay in Nashville during the summer and live with his friends at the house they all lived in which was called "The Hoose" (Leigh Ann and I could tell some stories about that place!). We told him if he worked full time, he could stay. Of course, the reasons he shouldn't have to work were immediately fired our way, including the fact that none of the other boys in the house had to get a job. We told him that was the only way he would be allowed to stay that summer, so he begrudgingly found a job doing grunt work for a production lighting company. It was dirty, sweaty, and exhausting. Little did he know that the people he met and worked for that summer would lead to one of the greatest experiences of his life a few years later when he went on tour with Luke Bryan as a lighting director. While it was not natural for him early in his life to work hard, our efforts of making Max have summer jobs and responsibilities at home led to him ultimately having a strong work ethic and opportunities later in life that he wouldn't have had otherwise. Having a willingness to work always pays off.

FINISHING STRONG

It seems like we've become a society where instant gratification is more important than being an honorable, responsible person. Contemporary thinking can lead us to focus on ourselves. It's common to hear things like:

- Don't I have the right to be happy all the time?

- If I have a bad day at work, then I just need to change jobs.

- If I don't like doing something, then I can just quit, even if it affects others.

- If my best friend and I have a fight, then I'll just find another best friend.

When I was growing up, the way to listen to music was to play an entire album at one sitting. Play side one, turn it over, and then play side two. When it was finished, I could listen to another record or go do something else. I remember being a young boy and sitting for hours, listening to Three Dog Night and Elvis and Johnny Cash (I've always had varying musical interests, and still do to this day). Watching my kids grow up during the age of iPods, Napster, and now streaming services, I've noticed that many in this younger generation not only don't listen to entire albums, but many times won't even listen to a single song from start to finish. I am a musician, and this bothers me from the standpoint of musical integrity, but

I think it is a symptom of the much bigger issue—the growing, constant need for immediate gratification that is so ingrained in our kids and our society overall.

As parents, we must fight against this trend towards instant gratification and teach our kids the concept of finishing what they start. If someone is always looking for the next great thing and isn't taking the time to appreciate and be dedicated to what he's doing in the moment, it is easy for him to become a person who is easily distracted and never truly fully committed. If your son signs up to play on a sports team, he should finish the season unless there's an injury. If your daughter auditions for a play at school and is chosen, she needs to stick with it, even if it's not as fun as she thought it would be. A summer job is for the entire summer, not just until boredom sets in or friends who don't work start going to the neighborhood pool every day.

Madeline tried many different activities: piano, soccer, volleyball, and dance. She didn't stick with all of them for a long time, but even when she wanted to quit one of them, we made her finish the season or semester that she had started. I remember when she was eight years old she wanted to quit piano right before her recital. She didn't love playing the piano, was tired of dedicating the time to take lessons, and had other stuff she'd rather be doing. We talked to her about why she had to finish the semester and made her play the recital. I can say that one of the fondest memories we have of her childhood was her dressing up in that clown costume and playing that recital, and almost twenty-five years later, her grandparents still talk about it. She had fun, we had fun, and it provided Madeline a small life lesson about finishing what she starts.

Another lesson that goes hand in hand with finishing what you start is the concept of counting the cost. Every potential commitment is an opportunity to help your children weigh the pros and cons of committing, and then they can make their own decision about whether or not they want to play that sport or get that job or do that thing. But once the commitment is made, the commitment should be fulfilled, and there really should not be an easy way out.

If your child makes a commitment to a team or to a program, that commitment impacts other people, and there are great lessons to be learned by finishing strong. It may not be the best thing in the world, or may not even be fun at all, but you gotta finish it. That is why a commitment is called a commitment. And just showing up is not in and of itself finishing a commitment. Sitting there on the bench with a bad attitude doesn't do anyone any good. Commitments require us to finish what we start and to finish with effort and with as much positivity as we can muster.

NO "FAILURE TO LAUNCH"

One sensitive subject regarding responsibility that I'd like to address is the current trend of post-college kids who are living at home for years after graduation. I know there are situations where this might be necessary for a time, but another saying we always had in our family was that there will be no "failure to launch." What we meant was that Leigh Ann and I were not going to enable our kids by allowing them to live at home indefinitely. They were required to grow up and become responsible adults who get jobs and provide for themselves. We made sure that Madeline and Max knew they were going to have to assume normal adult responsibilities when they became young adults and support themselves when the time came. If you slow the progress of your child becoming and acting like an adult, then you are being an enabler. It may seem like you are being helpful and loving in the moment, but you are actually putting them at a disadvantage over the long haul of their life.

If your child has a hardship or catastrophe in life, then absolutely be a supportive parent and take him or her in, helping to figure out what next steps are. It also might make sense for your son or daughter to live at home for a bit while beginning a career in order to save money for buying that first house. But if your child is thirty years old, doesn't want to work, and sits at home playing video games all day, then you as a parent are not parenting well by allowing that.

OLD-FASHIONED TALKING AND WRITING

Another aspect of teaching responsibility to your children is teaching them how to effectively communicate. In today's world, electronic communication is everything, but kids also need to know how to write a letter and how to stand up and greet an adult who walks in the room. They need to be able to carry on a fluent conversation with their teachers and other adults as well as their friends, and to be able to look them in the eye while they are speaking.

Electronic communication has severely stifled the ability of many of our young people to have a normal conversation, and that is sad. There is no question that texting and email is very useful, but our society has allowed electronic communication to almost totally replace verbal communication, which has created a lot of social awkwardness. The art of being able to effectively communicate verbally is quickly becoming a thing of the past, so it is imperative that we make sure our children are put in the position of having to actually talk to people in person, and to do so often. Whether it's speaking with a teacher about a bad grade or breaking up with a boyfriend or girlfriend, they need to be able to have important conversations verbally, effectively, and hopefully face-to-face.

Another form of responsible communication is responding to all emails and texts when received. I'm amazed that over the last decade or so our society has become a "respond if I want to and if it's convenient" society. There are many who think it's okay to regularly ignore people who communicate with them. I'm not saying a response to every sales solicitation or randomly received text from a stranger is necessary, but it seems the younger generation has lost the skill of responding promptly and even thinks it's okay to ignore messages they don't feel like answering. When you ignore people, it shows them a lack of respect, and people deserve to be shown honor, even in the seemingly small things.

Also, it may be old-fashioned, but I still believe our kids should call everyone a good bit older than they are "sir" and "ma'am" and "mister" and "missus." A teenager calling her friend's dad or mom by their first name fails to give them the respect they deserve. I'm almost sixty years old, and there are still many folks I call Mr. and Mrs.— and I will until the day they die. They deserve it.

BETTER LATE THAN NEVER,
BUT BETTER EARLY THAN LATE

Keeping to a schedule in a timely manner is another form of responsibility that seems to be a bit of a lost art. Children should be taught the importance of being on time, and this starts with them watching you consistently be on time. There's nothing that says someone or something is not important more than consistently showing up late, and it is a negative non-verbal cue to them. Of course, there might be circumstances where you can't avoid it, but showing up ten or fifteen minutes after church or ball practice starts is telling God or the team that they are not high on the priority list.

I once was asked if I would rather have to be ninety minutes early or thirty minutes late everywhere I went, and I didn't have to think one second about it—I'd rather be ninety minutes early. Otherwise, I would be insulting people left and right by showing up late. It is the responsible and honorable thing to be a little early or at least on time, and teaching this to your kids early in life by word and example will let them know its importance. Being on time is an important part of being a salt-of-the-earth human being!

Teaching our kids to be responsible is a difficult balance to strike. We naturally want our kids to like us, but some of the lessons we teach them about responsibility will create some tension and strife. Sometimes it's not comfortable or convenient to teach these lessons, and teaching our children to be truly responsible human beings is not the path of least resistance most of the time. The Apostle Paul says in Galatians 6:5 that "…each one should carry their own load," and there is so much wisdom in that broad but very impactful statement. If we don't work hard as parents to use every opportunity we have to help our children become responsible young people, then we will likely be setting them up to become irresponsible adults. Teaching our children the principles of responsibility helps them feel positive self-esteem, that their lives have meaning and purpose, and that they are making a difference in the world. Living a life of responsibility is living a grounded, respectable, salt-of-the-earth life.

TO CONSIDER:

1. Do your children have age-appropriate responsibilities in your household?

2. If old enough, do your children have "real" jobs? If your children are not old enough, do you plan for them to work when they can drive?

3. In what ways and situations is it important to you for your children to show honor and respect for others?

4. How does a sense of entitlement negatively affect someone's ability to be a responsible person? Any real-life family examples?

5. How much importance do you as a family place on "finishing strong?"

CHAPTER FOUR

DON'T ALWAYS COME TO THEIR RESCUE

"Though he may stumble, he will not fall...."
Psalm 37:24

A GUTTER BALL IS GOOD

Feeling protective of our kids is natural. We love them and always want the best for them. However, at times parents can be overprotective to a fault. If our kids rarely or never experience bad situations because we as parents act like bumpers in a bowling lane for them, their growth as humans will be stunted. They NEED to throw a gutter ball every now and then. Without bumpers, their bowling score won't always be as good, but eventually they will become better overall bowlers.

Every human being on earth will have challenging

circumstances at some point in their lives, and if we constantly shield our kids from seemingly bad situations, it could be harmful for them in the long run. If your child has always been protected, he or she will not know how to handle unpleasant situations, and this can lead to a life of anxiety and even depression down the road. So, your goal of keeping your kids from negative situations all the time while they are growing up can give them unrealistic expectations and possibly be the reason they end up having issues later on as an adult.

Parents have a natural instinct to rescue their children whenever possible. If our kids are unhappy, it's easy to feel like we are doing a bad job as parents. Allowing our children to experience negativity, which includes us having to experience their negative emotions that go along with it, can frazzle our own nerves, and we will naturally want to make the negative situation go away as soon as possible. This might help in the moment, but it also creates a long-term pattern that isn't good for anyone. Guiding them gently through these unhappy periods while still allowing them to experience and work through them will help develop children into more well-rounded and mature people.

AM I AN OVER-RESCUER?

What are the signs you may be an over-rescuer? Here are some possible indications:

- Do you find yourself doing whatever it takes to make your young child stop crying? For instance, if your three-year-old is unhappy and crying, do you immediately whip out the candy as a bribe to stop? Children's emotions are not the same as adult emotions, but it's easy to react to them as if they are adults. If we see an adult crying, then there's probably something very wrong, and we should do everything we can to help. If a child is crying, it's easy to react the same way, but it's rarely a critical emergency for the child—it's just them being a child. Crying for children is normal, and there will be times that it might be best to let them cry it out.

- Do you find yourself reacting all day long to whatever surface emotion your teenager is having and then doing anything you can to make him or her happier?

- Do you organize and reorganize your life so your children aren't "triggered" in any way? If you do, you are stunting their emotional growth and maturity. They will get used to you intervening and fixing the situation and will grow to expect it. Then, when they really do have to deal with something significant on their own, they might not be equipped to handle it.

- Do you constantly give in to your children's whims when it comes to a later bedtime or their desire to do various activities that you know aren't the best for them? Are they able to press and press until you do what they want you to do?

- Are you ready at the drop of a hat to get involved in any situation where you feel like the other kids on the playground or the teachers at school or coaches of the team are treating your child unfairly?

If you answered yes to any of the above actions, you might be an over-rescuer. If you find yourself always micromanaging your children in an attempt to make every angle of life smooth, even in the smallest things, it's time to resist the temptation and allow them to experience some of life's frustrations and challenges. Growth will come from it.

MACRO GOOD, MICRO BAD

When it comes to the day-to-day lives of your children, do you find yourself constantly managing the smallest details for them? If you do, you just might be one of those "helicopter parents" everyone has heard about. Hovering over your kids and overseeing and supervising every single aspect of their lives is a natural thing to want to do. It might make you feel like you are doing a good job as a parent, but you likely are doing more harm than good. It's a balancing act, and of course you should be actively involved in their lives. But managing every single detail and not allowing them to learn on their own prevents them from maturing and will cause some tough situations for them later in life.

Does your child forget things a lot? Maybe it's because you do too much remembering for them. If you let your daughter forget something she is supposed to bring to school and she gets in trouble for it, she is more likely to remember it the next time. If your son has a tendency to be late to practice, try reminding him to get ready once, but after that, allow him to be late. Then let him be the one to explain it to the coach. It may be difficult to be that hands-off at first, but allowing your child to experience the consequences of his actions (or inactions) will encourage him to become responsible and timely.

IT'S SOMEBODY ELSE'S FAULT

Over the many years I coached boys' lacrosse, it was easy to tell who the helicopter parents were. They were the parents who constantly complained directly to me (or behind my back) that their kids were not getting enough playing time. They would often make a blanket statement that it "just wasn't fair" that their son wasn't starting. It had to be that the coach (me) was playing favorites or just didn't like their son. Some of them would actually come over to the sideline and try to talk to me during the games. The real problem was that their son just wasn't playing as well as some of the other players. The parents then made the situation worse by blaming the coach rather than encouraging their son to work harder, having him ask the coach what he could do to gain more playing time, and encouraging him to be supportive of the "team" concept rather than the "me" concept. It perpetuated the thought in the boy's mind that everything was always someone else's fault, but the truth in life is it's usually not someone else's fault. Ultimately, that kind of thinking and parenting leads to narcissism and a sense of entitlement for the child.

I remember Sammy Dunn, the baseball coach when I was in high school, telling the team that if any parent ever came and talked to him about playing time for their son, then the boy was immediately off the team, no questions asked. That was probably too tough, but it sure let the boys know that they would have to make their own way when it came to the team. Once, a mother at one of the parenting small groups that Leigh Ann and I led was complaining that her five-year-old daughter's soccer coach wasn't giving her enough playing time and was hurting her chances to play professionally. I literally laughed out loud, thinking she was kidding, and then realized she was dead serious. Oh, how I felt for that little five-year-old girl.

HEY, TEACHER!

The parent/teacher/child relationship is a tricky one. All of a sudden, your children have another adult directly influencing their lives and spending more time with them during the day than you do. It's nothing new, but that doesn't change the fact that there will be times this three-way relationship will present some potentially difficult situations.

From what I've seen, many parents today think it's perfectly acceptable to storm up to the school and demand a teacher conference every time something goes wrong. If the child makes a bad grade, they accuse the teacher of writing the test incorrectly or of not teaching them well. If the child has to sit in the corner because of talking too much in class, then surely it's because the person next to them was talking too much. If he gets sent to the office for some reason, the parent insists there's a reason he shouldn't have been sent.

Sometimes, even though we don't want to believe it, our kids just make bad grades because they didn't prepare. Sometimes they really do talk too much in class. Sometimes they deserve to go to the office.

When other parents around you "over-parent" you might feel pressured to do the same, but allowing your children to work through tough situations will teach them to be much more able to deal with tough situations when they get out on their own. So instead of immediately demanding a teacher conference whenever there is a negative situation between your child and the teacher, try counseling your child about how to deal with it himself. Although there may be times when you need to intervene because of unfair treatment, a good life lesson is that life is not always fair.

When I was in grade school, the threat of getting paddled was constant. I'm not talking about a ruler on the hand, but a big wooden paddle wielded by one of the coaches or principals. I will say I got my fair share of licks from those paddles, some from the aforementioned Coach Dunn. And back then, if your parents found out you were paddled at school, you could expect to get punished again when you got home. Now, I'm not saying that paddling at school is the correct way to discipline, but I do believe the pendulum has swung too far the other way. Many times, instead of backing the authority of the school administration, parents defend their child in any situation, even if their child is in the wrong, and nothing ever seems to be the kid's fault.

Leigh Ann and I had a few times over the years where we so badly wanted to confront our kids' teachers, and it was all we could do not to do it. But before they ever started school, we made a rule for ourselves that unless our son or daughter was in danger or being bullied or attacked at school, we would never say one negative word to a teacher. We successfully held to that rule their entire school lives, and our kids were better for it from having to realize that actions really do have consequences, and Mom and Dad weren't going to get them out of them.

TEACHERS SHOULD TEACH AND PARENTS SHOULD PARENT

I do believe that parents should be involved in knowing what is being taught to their kids at school. Teachers aren't your kids' parents—you are. Teachers should stick to teaching math, science, history, and English, but today some schools are using teaching as a lifestyle-influencing platform. Please be aware of the curriculum being taught, and step in immediately if you feel there are some things that are not appropriate. If there are things that go against what you believe and what you stand for as a family, then by all means get involved in challenging and changing that. Nehemiah 14:4 says, "...Don't be afraid of them. Remember the Lord, who is great and awesome, and fight for your families, your sons and daughters, your wives and your homes." It's high time we step up the fight for influence on our sons and daughters, and this includes their elementary, high school, and college educations.

Life is not always fair. Whether it's not getting to eat a treat before dinner or not getting enough playing time on a youth sports team or not getting a job promotion at work, there will always be situations that just don't seem fair. Perhaps more important than the actual situation is how we teach our children to handle the situation. Sometimes, even in the early stages of their lives, we must let our kids experience discomfort and painful situations and then, with our guidance, allow them to process and work through these situations. Doing so will equip them to more effectively navigate negative situations as young adults and adults. Allowing our kids to work through problems leads to their developing problem-solving skills and teaches them how to deal with not just unpleasant situations but unpleasant people as well. If you allow your kids to navigate bad situations, with your counsel as needed, it doesn't make you a bad parent. It means you are parenting well.

TO CONSIDER:

1. What does the statement, "Without bumpers, their bowling score won't always be as good, but eventually they will become better overall bowlers," mean to you?

2. Do you feel you aren't being a good parent if you aren't involved in every detail of your children's lives?

3. Do you believe that the kids of today are being taught to have a victim mentality? If so, by whom?

4. How does experiencing disappointment or pain help a child to grow as a person?

5. Is your child's school teaching things that aren't in line with what you think should be taught at school?

CHAPTER FIVE

NO PAIN, NO GAIN

*"Whoever spares the rod hates their children,
but the one who loves their children is careful to
discipline them." Proverbs 13:24*

SPARE THE ROD?

To punish or not to punish, that is the question. Should punishment play a part in the raising of our kids, and if so, how big of a part? That's a tough question, and there are many schools of thought on the subject. In the verse above it says that if we don't discipline our children, we hate them, and if we discipline them, we love them. That's some strong language! I know hate is a harsh word, but I think since the wisest man who ever lived said it (Solomon), it's worth considering what he means in this verse and how it applies to our own family.

Today, many parents seem to err on the side of not punishing their kids, either because they don't want to have the hassle (to the parents) that punishing the child brings, or they want to make their relationship with their kids be more like friends than parents. After all, punishing is no more fun for the parent than it is for the children because you have to deal with their unpleasant reactions and the possibility of your schedule changing as well as theirs. But here's an immutable fact—you should be your child's parent first and friend second, and part of being a good parent is appropriately disciplining your children.

PARENT OR FRIEND?

The four of us had a lot of fun together as the kids grew up. When Madeline was young, we constantly played grocery store with her as the checkout person. I played hours and hours of various sports with Max. Madeline put makeup on us and "fixed" our hair many times. We had "Fun Club," consisting of indoor things like dodgeball and hide-and-seek, and "Trail Club," consisting of outdoor things like hiking and exploring. Leigh Ann and I would videotape them doing these crazy skits, and when they were little would laugh as they rode their first bikes in a loop inside our house from the den to the living room to the kitchen and back to the den probably a million times. Playing paintball and airsoft, running lemonade stands, riding the wagon full speed down our steep driveway, helping them build forts, and playing in the pool—we all had a lot of fun together.

Despite these great times, we were always their parents first, and part of being their parents was being disciplinarians. We would make sure to let our kids know what was expected of them, and if they did something wrong, we would encourage them to do better. If they did it again, they would likely be punished because we felt that it was so important for them to learn about actions and consequences.

DISCIPLINE

In general, Leigh Ann would take the lead with any discipline that was necessary, and then if I needed to get involved, I would. That worked best for us because she is a calmer person than I am and could generally make the best decisions when it came to punishment. Even though my Type A personality wouldn't want to, I tried hard to trust her instincts when it came to discipline. But if punishment was called for, then punishment it was, regardless of the inconvenience for us. And you can bet that not punishing would have been easier on us most of the time but would not have been the best thing for the child.

It's worthwhile noting that there's a difference between your children making a mistake and doing something wrong. Punishment should be reserved for intentional disobedience, like doing something they know they are not supposed to do or not doing something they know they are supposed to do. Making a mistake, like accidentally knocking over a glass of milk, isn't something to punish.

Both of my children had their own personalities and their own things they typically did to get in trouble. With Madeline, it was usually something to do with driving her brother crazy when they were both young, and as she got older it was mainly for her attitude. She has a lot of my personality in terms of stubbornness and saying exactly what she thinks, and between the ages of eleven and eighteen, she was a real pill!

With Max, his stuff was usually more stealthy. He ended up sneaking around and doing things that many boys do when they become teenagers, and he definitely became the family's most actively disciplined child in those years. I totally understood him, but Leigh Ann had grown up with no brothers and she just didn't understand why he did some of the things he did. His antics really bothered and upset her, so there were many times I took the lead with his punishment, having been a boy myself back in the day.

We always were able to deal with and work through the things they did, but to us the biggest of the big was lying. Lying was worse to us than anything they might have done that caused them to lie, and for it we had a zero-tolerance policy. I don't really know why Leigh Ann and I felt so strongly about that, but we did, and the kids always knew it. It might not have led to many changes in their behavior, but it definitely led to more honest discussions about what they did and a more sincere heart on their parts.

ACTIONS AND CONSEQUENCES

Even at an early age, we made sure our children knew about actions and consequences. From the time they were able to know the difference between right and wrong, we made sure to follow through with any punishment we threatened because not following through would let them know that their parents were able to be manipulated, and we didn't want them to play on that as they grew up. It's sometimes tempting to let your children talk you down a bit when you threaten punishment, but once you say it, as a parent you need to do it. Of course, you have to be very careful not to say anything that you know you shouldn't do or you don't want to do. Speaking in haste when it comes to punishment can put you in bad situations as a parent.

When my kids were young, punishment would be something like not getting to eat a popsicle or having to sit in time out—something age-appropriate. As our kids got older and the offenses got more consequential, their punishments got more consequential as well.

Max was a smart kid, and in the first semester of ninth grade, when grades really started to matter, he made three As and three Bs. That was fine, but he did that without really trying, so I encouraged him to put in a better effort in the second semester and make the best grades he could before high school got tougher. The idea was to pad his GPA early on so he would have a little powder left later in high school for the really tough classes.

I asked him a couple of times during second semester if he was putting in a good effort, and his answer was always yes. But I had a sneaking suspicion that wasn't the case. Still, I resisted the urge to constantly ride him about it because he knew what was expected of him. At the end of the second semester, I got his report card and he had made one A and five Bs. Now, if he had tried hard and made straight Cs, I would have been fine with that, but I knew he didn't try at all. He was rebelling against my asking him to put in a good solid effort. After leaving the house for a couple of hours because I was mad, I cooled off and finally decided that if he was going to act irresponsibly and immaturely like a child, then I was going to treat him like a child. Summer was just beginning, so I gave him a bedtime of 9:00 p.m. for the summer, just like I would for an eight-year-old instead of the fourteen-year-old he was. What made it worse for him was the fact that our swimming pool was right outside his bedroom window, and he got to listen to the entire neighborhood playing in our pool many nights. This may sound harsh to you, and he was really mad at me for it, but we rarely had another problem with him not putting effort into school. He ended up making very good grades the rest of high school and getting a full academic scholarship for college.

We tried, when possible, to make the punishment productive. For example, as a teenager, Max spent many hours painting furniture as his punishment. Madeline was asked to do more than her usual amount of house cleaning. After all, if they are being punished, they might as well be helping around the house.

WHAT ABOUT THIS "ROD"?

The verse at the beginning of this chapter mentions a "rod," and there are many schools of thought about what Solomon means. If taken literally, I would equate it to a paddle or switch in today's world. If taken figuratively, I would equate it to any form of discipline. With the latter, the rod could mean sitting in time-out or not having your phone for a week.

True spanking was way more of a thing when I was a boy than it is now, and it's hard to land on one rule or stance on this issue and be absolutely convinced it's correct. I am not against spanking when called for, but I personally believe it should be the exception rather than the rule. I believe that most of the time, punishment can be effective without spanking, but there may be times where it seems like spanking or the threat of spanking is the only thing that will change a certain behavior. In any case, I do wonder exactly what the Bible means in the "spare the rod" part of the verse.

I got a few bad spankings from my dad when I was

young, and I still remember every single one. Most of them were for disrespecting my mom, and one of them was for punching my sister in the face when I was about seven. I can guarantee the fear of being spanked made me behave better than I would have otherwise, but the spankings really didn't do anything to change my heart. Still, I turned out okay despite the spankings. I understand the reasons people are against spanking, and I believe that other forms of punishment are more effective most of the time. Personally, I never spanked Madeline and I only spanked Max once.

An uncomfortable part of the spanking subject is when and if it becomes abuse. There is no question that some (but hopefully few) parents get a power surge out of striking fear in their kids, and part of this equation can lead to physically abusive situations. If you are a spanker, then use it judiciously and sparingly, and never, ever, ever let it become what could be considered abuse. If you struggle with that in your anger, then just decide you are never going to spank.

FEAR VS. LOVE

It's interesting to think about why your children obey you when you ask them to. If your children act a certain way because they fear you, then their obedience will not be as meaningful as when their actions are based on the positive and loving relationship you have worked hard to build with them. If the trash needs to be taken out and the son knows dad will fly off the handle if he doesn't do it, then out of fear he'll take the trash out. If the trash needs to be taken out and the son knows his dad loves him and he appreciates all his dad does for him, then he'll take the trash out. Same result, different motivation. Parents, if you work hard to develop a deep, loving bond rather than a utilitarian bond between you and your kids, everything about parenting them will be easier. It says in 1 John 1:18 that "…perfect love drives out fear…" which means that love is a much deeper and more meaningful emotion than fear.

THE SPIRIT OF DISCIPLINE

Discipline should be firm but not overbearing or it will cause your children to be bitter towards you in the long-term. If your kids think of you—particularly you fathers—as a military sergeant when it comes to discipline, you are not handling discipline correctly. Colossians 3:21 says, "Fathers, do not embitter your children, or they will become discouraged," and a discouraged child is never a good thing. There is a healthy balance to be struck when it comes to discipline, because too much is bad and too little is bad. Just pray for clarity and judgment in every situation, and then follow your heart and follow through.

Consistency is also important when disciplining so that your children know what to expect. If they get the hammer for an offense one time and then nothing happens the next time they do the same thing, that will only lead to confusion. A big part of punishment is creating an understanding with your children about actions and consequences, and then having consistency between the message and the actions.

Also, please try not to discipline in anger or rage. If you find yourself furious about something, let your spouse handle the discipline or at least wait until you level out a bit in your emotions. One thing I have always struggled with is patience, and I tried hard (but not always successfully) not to discipline in anger because that is always counterproductive. I mentioned the story earlier about Max and his grades, and if I had engaged with him when I first got his report card, I would not have handled things appropriately. Instead, I decided to just leave the house and take a bit to think about the best way to handle that situation, and by the time I returned, I felt that the punishment I had decided on in my "cooling off period" was appropriate. If you find yourself too angry, take time to cool down, and then decide what the punishment will be.

WORDS MATTER

One thing that is never effective in punishment is being derisive in your language towards your children. Parents, please don't be demeaning in the language you use with your kids. Never ask them why they don't act as well as their sibling or friend, don't compare them negatively with someone else, and don't tell them they are a bad person in some way—they are a good person who did something bad. And never tell them they are stupid. Words matter, and how you deliver your message to them is extremely important.

There are times when raising your voice with your kids is necessary to make a point, but if you are constantly yelling at them, the impact is lessened, and they will get to the point where they don't hear you at all. ***Don't be a yeller!*** Make it a habit to have a legitimate conversation with them to ensure they understand why they are being punished so they can do better next time. If they don't understand why, and all they hear is yelling, they will not be able to learn from the punishment and eventually will tune you out altogether.

Also, please make sure to compliment your children often. I'm not talking about telling them they're the greatest every time they do something, but make sure to affirm and build them up, and do it often. Tell them you love them every single day, and show by action that no matter what, your love is unconditional. Also, always be a safe haven for your kids because they need to know that even if they blow it, they can come to you to talk about it. The ideal balance is having a relationship with your children where they will come talk to you, even though they know the outcome will likely be punishment.

Disciplining your children isn't fun and doing it appropriately will likely make your own life more difficult. Nobody likes seeing their child angry or sad or upset, but it will pay off for them in the long run if you consistently and thoughtfully discipline them. The world is harsh, and teaching your children about actions and consequences will help them become well-adjusted young adults when it comes time for them to be out on their own. Thoughtful discipline does not make you mean or a bad person or parent. Thoughtful discipline means that you are parenting well.

TO CONSIDER:

1. What does "spare the rod, spoil the child" mean to you?

2. What type of actions would most likely lead to punishment for your children?

3. What steps can you take when it comes to punishment to make sure you do not overly embitter your children towards you?

4. How are the words and tone of your language towards your children important?

5. Do you ever find yourself not punishing your children when they should be punished or find yourself letting offenses slide? If so, why?

CHAPTER SIX

IF YOU DON'T KNOW THEIR FRIENDS, YOU DON'T KNOW YOUR CHILDREN

"Do not be misled: Bad company corrupts good character." 1 Corinthians 15:33

THE INFLUENCE YIN AND YANG

When my kids were between the ages of three and ten, I remember thinking that Leigh Ann and I would always be the most impactful people in their lives. I mean, look at how we affect them and how they respect our authority! Then, as they approached age eleven or twelve, I started to sense that our impact was lessening and their friends were becoming more and more of an influence on them. By the time they got to high school, we provided meals and a roof over their heads, but at times that seemed to be about the limit of our influence—and not by our choice.

As I mentioned earlier, my son was the easiest baby I had ever been around, and his challenges came a bit later. As Max got older, he started hanging out with some friends who were good guys overall, but I was young once, and I was able to tell what they were likely up to. My instincts proved to be true later when Max's actions, in unison with the aforementioned friends, raised some situations in high school and college that were not fun for any of us, including Max.

Looking back, I'm not sure what, if anything, I would have done differently, because if I had been too harsh with him regarding his friends, I think it would have backfired. On the other hand, I probably should have paid more attention to what was going on and been a bit more strict about some of those friends. In any case, it's just one of those things for me that was difficult to know what to do in the middle of it, so I just made the best decisions I could with the information I had.

Even though I spent a ton of time with Max as he grew up, my influence waned as he got older and his friends' influence gained more and more traction at the same time. To use a mathematics term, it was kind of an "inversely proportional" thing when it came to who was doing the influencing the older he got.

Knowing that their friends will end up playing a major part in who your kids ultimately will become begs the question: "How do you get to really know their friends?" And I'm not talking about knowing them on a superficial level. I'm talking about going deep to know who they are as young people, what their values are, and what potential problems certain friendships may cause your children.

YOU REALLY DO NEED MORE FRIENDS (EVEN IF THEY'RE 30 YEARS YOUNGER)

From the beginning, we wanted our house to be where all the neighbors and all our children's friends wanted to hang out, and we very intentionally created that environment. It made our lives as parents busier and more chaotic since there were a bunch of neighborhood kids at our house seemingly twenty-four seven, but it was one of the best decisions we ever made in parenting and provided more awesome memories than I can count. We did this for a couple of reasons. Firstly, we enjoyed it a lot, but we also wanted to keep a pulse on what was happening with Madeline and Max and their friends on a regular basis.

We did make it a point to avoid interfering too much when they were hanging out with their friends—that is, unless the five or six neighborhood boys ganged up on Madeline. Then they got a full dose of Mr. Hines! We made sure to give our kids space but were always around and aware of most of what was going on.

Part of parenting well is looking for opportunities to be around your kids and their friends without being a nuisance—and your kids will tell you when you become a nuisance. Be willing to drive them places and to host events at your house. Be willing to chaperone school events and to be a team mom. Overall, your time with them is fleeting, and you must take advantage of every opportunity to spend time with them without it being awkward or weird. Spending time with your kids will give you access to spending time with their friends as well, allowing you to really get to know them and what they're about.

YOUR INFLUENCE ON THEIR FRIENDS

There are a lot of broken homes and marriages in today's world. There are single parents, blended families, and many unique and sometimes painful circumstances. Some of these situations may result in hurting kids, so please keep an eye out for young friends that may be going through a tough time and may need encouragement. You aren't their parent, but you may be able to share a wise word or provide your home as a sort of safe haven.

Think about it this way: if God gives us $1,000 worth of influence, He won't give us a $1,000 bill. He will give us $1,000 worth of quarters. We will consistently have situations all through life where we may get to spend a quarter on a situation, fifty cents on the next one, and so on. This includes opportunities to minister to our children's friends. Of course, we cannot overstep our bounds as we are not their parents, but we can surely make a difference in their lives if we keep our eyes and ears open.

Leigh Ann and I tried to look at the times we were able to spend around our kids' friends as ministry opportunities, and we were very fortunate to be able to have a positive influence on some of them by modeling what a successful marriage looks like. One night a teenage friend of Madeline's said to us with great sincerity, "I like coming over here because y'all like each other." Wow, that was very meaningful to us and showed us again how we as parents can speak life into our children's friends when they may not be getting a lot of positive influence at home.

There is no question that investing time getting to know your children's friends will pay off. We recently received an email from one of Madeline's friends. She said, "Hi Mrs. Hines! You were on my mind, so I wanted to reach out and tell you how much I appreciate everything you did for me. You and Mr. Steve were always so warm and welcoming and, now that I have kids, I hope to be that momma to their friends." We had not talked to her since their graduation twelve years ago, so to unexpectedly receive that message was wonderful, and it let us know that even though we weren't really thinking about it at the time, we had made a meaningful impact in her life.

THEIR FRIEND'S PARENTS

Whenever possible, it's also good to get to know the friend's parents. You can tell a lot about who a child is from who their parents are. Are they absentee parents who never know where their kids are or what they are doing? Are the parents always trying to hock their kids off on other people so they can go do their own thing? What's on their parents' social media accounts? Are they the "cool" parents who let fifteen-year-olds drink at their house? Having at least a moderate level of familiarity with the parents of your child's best friends will give you some insights into those friends.

When Max was in eighth grade, the dad of one of his friends wanted to take all the boys to Hooters. He was a nice guy, but there was no way I was letting this happen. I was the only dad who said no, but I wasn't going to sign off on my eighth grade son going to a place I wasn't comfortable with, particularly with someone I didn't really know. I knew my influence on things like that would lessen dramatically over the next few years, but while I still had the influence, I exercised it, regardless of what the dad or the other boys thought about my decision.

ALCOHOL

Unless you are the rare exception, the alcohol issue will come up probably sooner rather than later with your children. My personal belief is that it should never be okay for your child to drink before the legal age, if for no other reason than the law of the land says so. As a parent, it's important to speak with your children early in life about the dangers of drinking (DUI, drunk driving injuries, alcoholism, etc.) and be involved in their decisions on when and if to drink after (or before) the age of twenty-one. Excessive alcohol ruins a lot of lives, so if you teach them responsibility on this subject early in life, they are more likely to handle drinking responsibly later.

Another key to teaching the responsible use of alcohol is for parents to lead by example. Mom, if your kids see you buzzing on wine every day by the time they come home from school, then you are setting a bad example. Dads, if you are drinking excessively every weekend, then it is likely your son or daughter will take a cue from you when they are out on their own. I've studied this drinking issue a good bit, and I believe the Bible teaches that drinking in moderation isn't wrong, but drinking excessively and getting drunk is. Ephesians 5:18 says, "Do not get drunk on wine, which leads to debauchery. Instead, be filled with the Spirit." That sounds to me like a clear directive against excessive alcohol use. Issues with alcohol can be passed down generationally, and as a parent, you don't want to be part of continuing that curse. If you drink, set a good example, drink in moderation, and talk to your children early in life about alcohol.

FRIENDS, SOCIAL MEDIA, AND ISOLATION

Keeping tabs on your child's social media accounts and that of their friends is another good way to keep in the loop on things. It's amazing how the under-developed ten- to twenty-year-old brain will put stuff on social media that they never should, and that can let you know what you need to know about certain friends and certain activities. Was there a big party with drugs and alcohol this weekend? Does your child's friend have an older brother with a questionable past who lives at home? Is someone bullying your child? Social media can be pure gold in the friend information department.

A concerning trend in today's society is that more and more kids are isolated and really don't have true friends. With the proliferation of electronic entertainment such as video games, the Internet, and social media, it's common for kids to be physically isolated from their peers. They feel like they are getting their social needs met through the computer and phone, and COVID-19 sure didn't help. Kids can establish their own world online and feel like they are meeting the innate need for social interaction that God placed in us all, but nothing can be further from the truth.

If you notice that your child is withdrawn and spending hours in the bedroom on the phone or laptop or becomes uninterested in things that used to be of interest, please take that very seriously. Talk about it and encourage joining a sports team or an extra-curricular activity. Invite a friend over or go to a church youth group activity. Your child may not want to, but sometimes as a parent you need to force this issue because there are consequences for inaction. If you feel that it is becoming a very serious problem, it may require seeking professional help. Lack of real, face-to-face interaction will stunt a child's emotional growth and lead to big problems later in life when faced with the adult world.

Also, childhood depression is a very real thing, and too much alone time and isolation allows it to develop into a big problem. A recent study in Psychology Today stated that the rates of loneliness are sharply rising among the young who increasingly report having no close friends, and this can be a major factor in leading to depression.[4] If our children are alone too much and not filling the needs they have for actual human contact, their minds can start

---

4 "Causes of Depression." Psychologytoday.Com. Psychology Today, January 21, 2023. https://www.psychologytoday.com/us/basics/depression/causes-depression.

playing tricks on them and causing some pretty serious emotional distress. Plus, a lack of human interaction and too much screen time creates a false sense of reality where it's easy to confuse an electronic world with what is actually real and true.

When Madeline and Max were young, we made them do simple things to encourage real, human-to-human interaction. For example, we had them call and place any take-out orders for pizza or for Chinese food. They really hated it at the time, but that simple interaction of speaking on the phone and ordering the food was a small step toward interacting with adults. At times we'd even take them with us to pick up the food, give them the credit card, and make them go in and pay. Another way to encourage social interaction is to have your kids go to your next-door neighbor to pick up something you are borrowing. Make them call their coach to tell them they are sick and can't be at practice instead of doing it for them. Have a standing play date with a friend. Make them call or go see their friend to have an important conversation rather than just texting. Have them schedule an appointment with the teacher to discuss something face-to-face, rather than sending an email. Whatever the case, just make sure your kids are having consistent, substantial, real human interactions.

FIGHTING WITH FRIENDS

What do you do when your child has a serious argument with a friend? When your child is involved in a conflict, talk to him about the best ways to resolve it, and then try to stay in the background and let him settle it. It may not be a friendship worth saving, but if it is, don't let him take the easy way out and just write the friendship off. Teach that friends are important and working through conflict is a part of life.

No one, including your children, should depend on messaging and texting to resolve conflict. Too much can be lost in translation, and things tend to be said via text that would never be said in a real conversation. When there's an issue, have your children talk to their friends in person or at least on the phone, and talk about what the issues are and how to fix the situation. It may sound a little old-school, but it is much more effective to resolve conflict through actual conversations rather than through instant messaging.

Also, please avoid the temptation to gossip about the fight with other parents. Parents tend to take much longer to forgive and forget than their kids do, and gossiping about someone else's child will (unfairly) cast him or her in a more negative light to other grownups than they deserve.

DECISIONS, DECISIONS

Parenting well requires some tough decisions, and you may need to make some difficult judgments concerning your children's friends.

It is okay to say no to your children spending the night with someone you don't know or is questionable. It is okay not to let them go to events that you don't feel comfortable about, even if everyone else is going. It is okay to say no to things if you aren't comfortable with their friend's parents. It is okay to end detrimental friendships for your children, even if they don't like it. Of course, this gets harder as they get older, but just remember that parenting is not about being popular with your child; it's about being good parents and doing what you feel is best for them.

TRUST YOUR GUT

When it comes to your children's friends, trust your gut—it will almost always be right. Many times, the Holy Spirit will speak to us in a whisper through "little voices" in our heads, but if you listen closely, that whisper will be as loud as a roar. You can call it your instinct or your intuition, but you know what I'm talking about. It's that voice that tells you something deep down inside that you know you need to listen to.

One time, when Leigh Ann and I both had serious reservations about Max spending the night in eighth grade with a boy we didn't know, we went against our strong instinct and let him go anyway. Well, sure enough, they ended up getting picked up by the police at two o'clock in the morning because they were walking on the side of a major road after they snuck out of the house. We should have listened to our gut and not been afraid to follow the instinct not to let him go. On another occasion when he was older, we had the same thing happen with a camping trip he and a couple of buddies were going on. Leigh Ann and I both felt the strong, seemingly out-of-the-blue prompting that he shouldn't go, and we told him that. He convinced us that it would be okay, and without going into all the details, that camping trip ended in disaster. To this day, we talk about the prompting we received about that camping trip, the lack of standing our ground after the prompting, and the bad results afterwards.

If you have a sneaking suspicion about one of your child's friends, do a little investigation and—more times than not—you will be right. If you find out something that needs to be acted on in some way, do it. Don't be lazy or detached when it comes to your children's friends and the issues in their relationships, because a lack of action (the old "path of least resistance") can have bad long-term consequences. There are countless stories of parents who wish they had never allowed certain friendships to form because those friendships eventually led to disaster. Those parents knew early on that the friendship was not a healthy one but ignored it and did nothing about it until it was too late. Little things can easily and quietly become big things, and dealing with them when they are little is much easier than ignoring them until they become big.

Even at a young age, knowing who your children's friends are is very important. As they grow older, it becomes even more important. In many ways, friends can shape who your kids turn out to be more than you as parents do, so don't underestimate the importance of their friend relationships. And remember—you as a parent can tell a lot about who your child really is from who their friends are. If the friends behave and act responsibly, chances are your child does, too. If the friends are wild, then it's likely that your child is as well, even if you don't see it.

Create opportunities to get to know your children's friends, be vigilant in keeping a healthy but watchful eye on their friend relationships and be diligent in dealing with any issues that arise from these friendships. Who their friends are will impact their lives possibly more than anything else, so being involved in helping them manage and guard their friendships will greatly impact who your children ultimately become.

TO CONSIDER:

1. Do you remember friends from your childhood who were bad influences on you? Were there any long-term effects?

2. As a parent, do you find that you make decisions based on the convenience or inconvenience the decision might have on you personally?

3. Is underage drinking okay with you?

4. What do you think about the issue of isolation with kids today?

5. Do your children currently have any friend relationships that you feel they would be better off without?

CHAPTER SEVEN

BOYFRIENDS
AND GIRLFRIENDS

*"Marriage should be honored by all, and the
marriage bed kept pure...." Hebrews 13:4*

DATING: SHOULD WE BE INVOLVED?

Oh, the dreaded topic of boyfriends and girlfriends!
I'm sure you remember your first "love" and how that
person made you feel and act and the sway he or she had
over you. A boyfriend or girlfriend will probably be the
biggest influence your child ever has, and those feelings
can start early.

As strange as it sounds, I remember being very smitten
by a girl in first grade, and I also still remember the phone
number of my fifth grade "girlfriend" fifty years later. I
only had one real girlfriend before Leigh Ann because I

was too into sports, but I remember those young love feelings—and they were very powerful.

Sometimes parents don't consider the importance of their children's dating life and who their boyfriends and girlfriends are. It's easy for parents to become casual observers as their children go through the dating process, not questioning or challenging some of the decisions that their teenage children might be making. Some parents neglect to establish ground rules for dating, and have a "hands-off" approach when it comes to this side of their child's life.

It is my contention that parents absolutely should be involved in helping young people make wise decisions about who they are dating, and to help them understand the importance of the dating relationship. Eventually, it's likely that one of the people they date will be the person they marry, and that will affect them one way or the other for their entire life. Other than a personal faith decision, who your child marries is the most important decision he or she will make, and relatively robust involvement and counsel from the parents can help them make a good one.

STYLES OF DATING

As I see it, there are two basic styles of dating. The first one is "courtship dating." The concept behind courtship dating is that marriage is a lifetime commitment and it should be treated with the level of importance such a major decision deserves. Because of the importance, the dating and marriage decisions under this model involve both the child and their parents equally.

One of my best friends, Ken Polk, utilizes the courtship dating model for his four kids, and it has worked well for them so far. In their family, Ken and his wife Ashley are the gatekeepers and scouts for who their kids end up dating. That means the kids rely on Ken and Ashley to ultimately decide if the person they are interested in is the right person for them to date. As they get older, the joint decision is made with the anticipation of them potentially marrying that person.

To assist in this courtship process, one of the most important steps Ken and Ashley take is creating a marriage filter with the child's input. In this process, they all get together before dating ever starts and list the desired qualities of a potential marriage partner. Then, until the child has met someone he or she could likely marry—someone who meets their filter—the child agrees to date only in group settings. This of course leads to group dating only all through high school and at least into the early college years. The child also agrees not to date any one person for more than three months at a time, at least until finding the person who is a serious contender for marriage. If the child does find someone he or she could marry, that person is then assessed through the filter as a potential marriage partner by both the child and the parents.

Courtship dating is not the method of dating most of us are familiar with, but it does deserve consideration within your family dynamic. And, for the kids to be on board, this style of dating must be discussed early in life. Parents have their child's best interests at heart, and for a child to trust that enough to allow a parent to be involved in the ultimate marriage decision can be very beneficial and quite cool. If you think this style would work for your family, there is much information on the Internet for you to explore and consider. For some kids, the style of courtship dating may be effective, but as with most things, kids are not "one size fits all."

The other style of dating is the style most of us are familiar with, where a young person dates around in high school and college, hoping to eventually find the person he or she will end up marrying. Get a boyfriend or girlfriend, date them as long as you want to, and then move on to the next if it doesn't work out. You might date someone for two weeks or for five years, and the thoughts about marriage happen when you have been with someone long enough to start thinking this may be a good person to marry. The decisions are all left up to the one doing the dating, without a large amount of involvement from the parents. It's the process I went through and also the process my kids went through, and they both have ended up with wonderful spouses.

CAN WE REALLY HAVE A POSITIVE IMPACT ON OUR CHILDREN'S DATING LIVES?

No matter what style of dating your family chooses, it is extremely important for you as parents to be involved in the thought processes your child goes through when deciding who they will date. Does the person have a strong moral compass? Are they Godly? Are they easily swayed by peers? Do they treat their parents well? Leigh Ann has always said you can tell a lot about a person by how they treat animals and babies, and I think there is a lot of wisdom in that. Active discussions between you and your children as they approach the age of dating is critical for them to be able to make some mature decisions when they start dating.

It is also important to make sure your children know the boundaries and expectations you have for them before they ever start dating, because once it starts happening, it happens fast. Map out guidelines and discuss them so everyone is on the same page, and always keep an open line of communication. It's important for the family to decide what the boundaries are before the kids start dating, and for the kids to feel that they had input in those decisions so they will more easily buy into what is decided. Decide about boundaries on things such as what age they can start dating, acceptable age gaps between themselves and those they date, when they can go on solo dates, and what they can do and where they can go on dates.

As with every relationship, communication is key. As a parent, work hard to nurture the relationship you have with your sons and daughters so they feel comfortable talking to you about issues with their boyfriends and girlfriends. When it comes to dating, they should have no better sounding board than their mom and dad, and the same is true about any aspect of their lives. While conversations will always be somewhat limited and perhaps uncomfortable because you are their parents, doing everything you can early in life to make them feel safe talking to you is critical.

Dads, you also should sit down and have a man-to-man talk with any boy who wants to date your daughter so he knows your expectations as well. In many ways, the boy drives the relationship in teenage dating. If a sixteen-year-old boy makes some commitments to the father about how he is going to treat his daughter, then that boy is much more likely to treat the girl with respect. Boys at that age have raging hormones, but when it comes to dating your daughter, if they know what you expect going in, they will have a much higher chance of acting appropriately.

WHEN AND WHO TO DATE?

What is an appropriate age to start dating under the more common dating model? Well, Leigh Ann was fifteen when we started dating, so that's the magic age! Of course, I'm saying that tongue-in-cheek. I think it varies according to the child's maturity, but in my personal opinion, I'd probably say a reasonably mature seventeen- or eighteen-year-old is probably ready for full-fledged dating to begin.

Before that age, just hanging out and some group dating should suffice. Leigh Ann and I met in the church youth group, and we were friends for a good while before our first date two years later.

But waiting until age seventeen or eighteen to start dating isn't always realistic. Social media and texting have made our children grow up fast, and they can practically communicate twenty-four hours per day, making relationships develop very quickly. I remember having to call Leigh Ann on her home phone if I wanted to communicate at all, and her parents knew exactly how long we talked because the phone was right in the middle of their kitchen. Our communication was basically limited to when we were together, and there was no texting or video chatting. Today there is a new dynamic with the change in how our children can communicate. After including your child in the conversation, decide what age is right for your child to date, and then stick to it.

DON'T BE AFRAID TO SWING YOUR SWORD

Sometimes as a parent you may have to make some drastic decisions regarding your children and their dating. Madeline's first boyfriend was a guy who hung out at the next-door neighbor's house a lot, and when she was fifteen, they suddenly fell into a boyfriend/girlfriend relationship. I wasn't thrilled about it, but I watched them as closely as possible for a few months while it went on. Early on, I felt his intentions toward Madeline were too physical, and right out of the gate I struggled with whether to let it go on or not. Leigh Ann and I prayed for God to reveal anything we needed to know, and boy, did He. It was amazing how specifically He answered that prayer, and things about their relationship quickly began to come to light in the most unexpected ways. When this happened, I put an end to their relationship and made them break up. Talk about an intense situation! I think Madeline literally hated me, Leigh Ann was questioning if I made the right decision, and the boy and his father on separate occasions drove to my house to beg me to let them stay together. It was a huge mess, but I felt the conviction of the Holy Spirit that I was doing the right thing. As Leigh Ann likes to say, I "swung my sword and chopped some ears off," and I didn't care one bit what any of them thought. This was my baby girl, and I would protect her at all costs. I was easily the least popular person around for a while, but soon after that happened, she met the love of her life, Zac Olinger, who is now my son-in-law. Zac is one of the best young men I've ever known, and I could not be happier to have him married to my only girl and to be the father of our two (and counting) granddaughters, who are a huge joy in our lives. Who knows who Madeline would be with today if I hadn't stood up for what I knew was right? I thank God for giving me the conviction and confidence in making that decision.

SEX AND DATING

Today, sex outside of marriage is more glorified and accepted than ever before, and doing what makes you feel good no matter your age is the norm. The world says if you want to experiment, then go ahead—that's your right. If you make a mistake, just get an abortion. If you want to live together and take a test drive before getting married, then that's fine. Just watch most television shows or streaming services or even mainstream TV commercials and you will know exactly what I mean. I honestly can't believe what is on commercials during prime time shows on the major channels—some of the most deviant stuff you can imagine that twenty years ago would have been relegated to R-rated movies, and it saddens and disgusts me. The constant sexuality portrayed in the media and the misguided messaging that goes along with it goes totally against God, and that is very disappointing to me.

For the Hines family, we are a Christian family, and we try to base every decision we make on Christian principles. Matthew 19:5 says, "For this reason a man will leave his father and mother and be united to his wife, and the two will become one flesh." I believe God makes it clear that His plan is for sex to be between a man and a woman within the confines of marriage. I know that sounds more old-fashioned than ever and goes against the grain of modern thinking, but I'm going to filter what I believe through the Bible, not through my preferences.

On the other side of the coin, if you don't agree with these lifestyles that are celebrated despite being outside of God's framework, you will be called a bigot and hateful and every other name imaginable. The pressure of society on this issue makes it tempting to just accept what's being spewed or at least to ignore it as best you can, but the Word of God trumps any opinion of man. In 1 Corinthians 4:3-4, it says, "I care very little if I am judged by you or by any human court; indeed, I do not even judge myself. My conscience is clear, but that does not make me innocent. It is the Lord who judges me." The basic message of this verse is that the opinions of other people or even your own opinions on an issue don't matter. What matters is God's opinion that He lays out in the Bible, and that is true about this issue of sex and sexuality, as well as any other issue. So, please don't ever let people make you feel bad about standing up for what you know to be true after sifting it through what God has to say about it in His Word.

Abstinence until marriage is not at all popular these days, and your children's friends will call them a prude or lunatic if they decide that they will wait for sex until they get married. But your kids need to know that's okay. As a family, it is very important to instill in your children the value of not letting society dictate what the rules are, and to not let society pressure them into bad decisions just because it's the popular thing to do. Society has a very loud voice, so teach your children early in life to ignore it and to stand up to the voices and bad outside influences that will want to take them down a path that they should not go.

Now, I am a realist, and I know that it's difficult to stick to keeping sex within the confines of marriage during those dating years. For thousands of years, Satan has exploited sex more than anything else, and quoting Biblical scripture will only go so far in keeping what is happening in the backseat of a car in check. If your children do agree to wait, let them know it will honor their future spouse in a way nothing else can. It will also keep them out of bad situations, such as unplanned pregnancies or STDs, and keep their reputation intact. That's why having clear discussions with your kids about sex is so important. Along with teaching these principles comes the principle of grace from you when they mess up.

Sex and dating is extremely hard to navigate for parents because kids can live promiscuous lives without us having a clue. Over a decade ago, the mother of one of my lacrosse players told us she caught him with nude pictures of his relatively young girlfriend on his phone, and it blew my mind. It was 2010, and I did not realize that sexting was as prevalent as it was. Well, it's way worse now. This whole sexting thing is more common than most parents realize, particularly with apps such as Snapchat, where pictures can disappear eight seconds after they are posted. There's also the huge issue of "sextortion," where people who only sent one or two objectionable pictures can be blackmailed and possibly ruined for life. Parents must learn to monitor for sexting, talk to their children about guarding against it, and get the children to commit to not being involved in it. Otherwise, kids will become sexually

SALT, LIGHT, & KIDS

"mature" way too fast. Kids of today are seeing and learning about things at age eight or ten that older generations didn't see or learn about until well into the teen years, and their young minds are in no way equipped to handle it. That is very frightening for the parents of today.

ABUSE IN DATING

Mental and sexual abuse is something to watch out for in your child's dating, and I believe it is more common than ever. A study by dosomething.org states that one-third of adolescents today are victims of sexual, physical, verbal, or emotional abuse in dating[5]. Here are some warning signs you can watch out for as parents:

- Is your child suddenly making bad grades or unwilling to talk to you about certain things?

- Is he or she suddenly acting distant?

- Does your daughter have unexplained marks or bruises?

- Is your child's boyfriend or girlfriend making

---

5 *"11 Facts About Teen Dating Violence." Dosomething.Org. Dosomething. Org, January 21, 2023. https://www.dosomething.org/us/facts/11-facts-about-teen-dating-violence.*

them slowly withdraw from friends or family?

- Is your child's boyfriend or girlfriend heavily influencing what your child attends or participates in?

Any level of abuse from either party is unacceptable, and abuse typically only gets worse as time goes on. Be on the lookout for any signs of abuse, whether physical, sexual, verbal, or mental. It can affect your kids for a lifetime, and it's up to you to do everything you can to guard against it, even after they are married.

Helping your children navigate their dating years is one of the most important and potentially difficult assignments you will ever have. For your kids, dating and the decisions centered around it are some of the most critical decisions they will ever make in their lives. Pray for clarity as a parent, be firm but have a level of grace, and hold on as best you can for the wild ride. You may want off the ride, but don't give up! Your child needs you during the dating years probably more than at any other time.

TO CONSIDER:

1. Do you feel that parents who want to have input on their kids' dating choices are overstepping their bounds as parents?

2. How do you feel that the world's view on sex has changed over the last twenty years? What effect does this have on your children?

3. How do you personally feel about sex outside the confines of marriage for your children?

4. What are your thoughts on the "courtship" style of dating?

5. How important is it for parents to have candid conversations with their children about the many important aspects of dating? Do you do this or plan to do it at the appropriate time?

CHAPTER EIGHT

THE CURSES OF MODERN TECHNOLOGY

"Be alert and of sober mind. Your enemy the devil prowls around like a roaring lion looking for someone to devour." 1 Peter 5:8

SATAN IS A MASTER OF DECEIT

It's amazing how Satan can take something good and turn it into something bad or impure. He may not totally remove the good aspects, but he is very skilled at twisting those good things into something bad.

Think about money or sex. By themselves, those are good things. God gives us money to be able to support our families and to help others, and He gives us sex as a wonderful part of a marriage. But Satan has turned both into something that, in many respects, is unclean. The perversion of sex in today's society, the obsession with material things—it's a corruption of what would be otherwise pure.

Satan is a master at slowly desensitizing our minds over time and making things that were at one time bad or sinful become accepted or even embraced. Think about the film *Gone with the Wind*. In the film, Clark Gable famously says, "Frankly, my dear, I don't give a damn." When the film came out in 1939, the reaction from almost everyone was shock and horror. Nobody could believe that an actor said the "D" word in a movie. Fast forward to today when films not only use the "D" word, but also commonly use every other curse word and regularly depict all kinds of filth. Primetime network TV regularly has cursing, extremely suggestive language, violence, and even sex. I've watched College Football GameDay for years on Saturday mornings and have noticed over the last year or two that the hosts now curse on their broadcasts. Even some news anchors use profanity. Unfortunately, it's shrugged off or not even noticed by most people, including some Christians.

Back in the days of Moses, when the Israelites finally went into the Promised Land, God told them to destroy the Canaanites (the modern culture of the land). Instead, they mingled with them and adopted their customs. God was very disappointed because His people didn't take a hard stand against the pagan culture as He had commanded. Instead, they became a part of it. I believe the same situation, in many ways, is occurring with some Christians today who do more blending in than standing against.

James 1:26 says, "Those who consider themselves religious and yet do not keep a tight rein on their tongues deceive themselves, and their religion is worthless." That verse doesn't require a lot of guesswork and interpretation. Bad language goes against what Jesus stands for, and we should be held accountable to keep our speech clean and wholesome. If your normal everyday language is a little crass or crude, please make a point to clean it up. Your kids will notice.

Satan has been masterful over the years in numbing our senses little by little. He's done it with sex, money, and language, and his main weapon has now become technology, media, and the Internet.

GIVE ME ANOTHER HIT

I can do a lot of what my daily life requires using my laptop or my phone. I can stay in touch with friends and family way more than I could before, and I can find out anything about anything with the push of a few buttons. I can find out all the daily news and keep up with everything about my beloved Alabama Crimson Tide in almost real time. Yet, with those same buttons I can quickly and easily get into some very harmful territory.

Dopamine is something that is associated with both mental and physical pleasure. Basically, it's a chemical in the brain that makes you feel good. Cocaine and meth give your mind a dopamine hit. Sex gives your mind a dopamine hit. If you're hungry and then you smell and eat chocolate chip cookies—same result. But did you know the entire premise of social media is built on having these same types of dopamine hits? If you get a like or a retweet, your brain responds with a dopamine pleasure sensation. And don't think that's by accident. The founders of all the big social media companies know this and build their platforms for maximized dopamine hits to the users' brains, thus keeping their users on the platform longer. And make no mistake—if you are on a platform that is free and you don't pay for any products, then you are the product. If these platforms can get you addicted to that dopamine rush, then they will be able to influence you in terms of your behavior without you even knowing it. What ads you see, what you read, and what pops up in your feed are all controlled by them.

REAL TALK ABOUT SOCIAL MEDIA

While social media does provide some useful services, it also has many aspects that can ultimately be disastrous for both you and your children. While it's not all bad, unchecked social media use, even at an early age, can result in some negative things such as an overly distracted mind, decreased emotional sensitivity, unrealistic views of others, bullying, lack of sleep, and depression. Recently I read about something called TTUD (TikTok Use Disorder), and I wasn't surprised at all to learn that apps are actually making us sick. As we all know, social media can be very addictive, and an addiction to anything is never good. Leigh Ann and I have concluded that we wish social media had never been invented because it seems the bad far outweighs the good, particularly with our young people.

When I was in grade school, bullying was a problem, but it was an occasional problem that was typically re-solved by a fight at the flagpole after school if you were a guy, or not letting an out-of-favor friend sit at the lunch table if you were a girl. Today, social media has made it easy for kids (and adults) to bully from afar, and for large groups of people to gang up on an unfortunate person with a level of meanness and vitriol that is disturbing. It's much easier for a bully to hide behind a keyboard and say things he or she wouldn't say face-to-face. Cyberbullying can destroy a child's self-esteem, and in the more extreme cases, can result in kids hurting themselves or even ending their life.

It's important as a parent to be aware of your children's social media activity, limiting the amount of time they spend on it and the number of social platforms they are allowed to be on. I encourage you to use filters to monitor your children's activity, and let them know you are doing it. Set screen time limits and talk to your kids about responsible social media use and participation. Make sure they understand that what they type can hurt people, including themselves. If you stop and think about it, the Internet is really written in permanent ink, and once something is out there, you can't take it back.

A VIRTUAL OPEN-AIR DRUG MARKETPLACE

Did you know that buying drugs on the Internet and

social media platforms is about as easy as tying your shoe? It's insane how easy it is for a kid to buy almost anything they want on the Internet, and even hard drugs are literally a click away. Name a drug and your child can find it on the Internet. To make matters worse, the mostly Chinese raw material producers and Mexican drug cartel manufacturers are now lacing many things with fentanyl, which can mean instant death. Kids think they are taking a Xanax they bought on Facebook to be cool, and then drop dead because they really took a fentanyl-laced pill. Drug buyers and sellers use very common emojis that correspond with specific drugs, and the dealers are all over social media. This is a problem that all parents must pay strict attention to, and you must talk to your kids about it. Tell them the dangers of taking anything, particularly something off the Internet or from someone they don't know, and don't feel bad about snooping around their social feeds or their bedroom a bit. Two of the lacrosse players that I coached died from opioids before they were twenty years old, and another one went through serious heroin addiction and treatment. Getting a call that your well-adjusted, high achieving kid has just died of an overdose is becoming more common with each passing day, and a lot of these situations are being caused by the drug markets on the Internet and social media.

THE STEALTHY UPCOMING SOCIAL DISASTER: GAMBLING

Internet gambling is another problem that I believe is much larger than most people realize. Gambling is another activity that releases dopamine, and the Internet makes it very easy to get involved. In the past, you had to call and place a bet with a bookie and then meet him in an alley to either collect or pay up. Today, there are many gambling options on the Internet such as DraftKings, and you can place bets, pay, and collect money all through an app. The casino is now on your phone, and well-respected people like football's Manning family are pushing gambling apps hard. Caesars has a series of ads featuring Peyton, Eli, Cooper, and Archie Manning pushing the Caesars gambling platform, and it bothers me that such well-respected people are endorsing an activity that can wreak so much havoc. Interestingly, not long after their initial ads, one followed about responsible gambling and what to do if you have a gambling problem, and I have to think they had an "aha moment" about it all after the first commercials came out.

Like many other things, what was once underground is now mainstream. I see the "first bet risk free" ads all the time and can easily see through the scheme the gaming companies are using to get people hooked. And don't underestimate the addictiveness of gambling because it has ruined countless lives. Unfortunately, now young people as well as adults can start hardcore gambling early in life with the click of a few buttons. The "house" knows that and is taking great advantage.

SEX ON OVERDRIVE

The sexualization of the Internet and the media makes my heart hurt. With a couple of clicks, anyone can find as much sexual perversion as they desire. This was not always the case, but now anything imaginable is a finger tap away. Porn is a multi-billion-dollar industry, and I feel sorry for our kids and for the parents raising them because it's almost impossible to prevent them from becoming sexually knowledgeable and exposed to graphic images at a very early age. If you don't have "the talk" early, you will be too late.

This hyper-sexualization of the Internet and media over the last decade or two distorts reality for everyone who allows themselves to be exposed to it, and exposure can lead to an overwhelming world of sexual fantasy. It can also lead to dissatisfaction in marriage because there may not be the same dopamine hit with a spouse that is achieved through things watched on TV and pornography. Biblically speaking, sexual sin is a biggie. In 1 Corinthians 6:18, it says, "Flee from sexual immorality. All other sins a person commits are outside his body, but whoever sins sexually, sins against their own body." In the most famous sermon of all time, the Sermon on the Mount, Jesus makes it clear that sexual sin includes our eyes and minds sinning, and not just physical actions. In Matthew 5:28, Jesus says, "But I tell you that anyone who looks at a woman lustfully has already committed adultery with her in his heart." Allowing our minds to think and dwell on these things is actually committing sexual sin, just as if we had committed the physical act of adultery. Whether it's sexting, porn, sexual predators, or females clothed in almost nothing on Instagram and TikTok, sexualization is a huge problem that runs deep in the fabric of our modern society. And let's be real: many adults are dealing with these issues themselves. As parents, it's important to lead by example and talk about the dangers of rampant sexuality and pornography with our children.

Protecting your kids from harm is a huge responsibility, and when it comes to sex, children are being exploited in ways that once were unimaginable. I personally know a young lady who, a few years ago, felt like she was being followed while shopping at Target. After feeling very uncomfortable for probably half an hour, she let store management know. After reviewing the security tapes, they were able to determine that the people she thought were following her around the store were known sex traffickers. That really brought home to me the fact that you can never be too careful. There are several public record internet sites that list sex offenders, and I suggest that parents do a quick internet search of any living nearby. You never know what you might find, and you don't ever want to be the parent who wishes they had done more.

WHAT IN THE WORLD
DO WE DO WITH ALL THIS?

What do we do with all this technology and social media when it comes to parenting? The most important thing to do is the same with all other aspects of parenting: communicate with your children. Talk to them about the dangers of the Internet and social media, and see what they have to say. As I previously mentioned, they can hide many things from you if they want to, regardless of your best filtering efforts, so having an open and honest discussion about the perils of the Internet will go a long way toward keeping your child grounded and safe.

Also, decide when they can get a phone before they ever get to the age when they would expect it. This can vary by child, but I recommend erring on the side of caution. Once they have their phone, their world will change dramatically, so don't feel pressure just because their friend got a phone at age eight. Decide what age works best for getting a phone for your child, and then stick with it. Once they do get a phone, set boundaries on screen time, and do whatever you feel necessary to keep tabs on both screen time usage and where they go on the Internet. You're not snooping—that's your right as a parent.

When it comes to the battle for purity in the media and on the Internet, there is not a whole lot we individually can do other than pray for hearts to be convicted. However, one thing I do to actively fight against the bad stuff I notice is any time I see a very offensive ad or commercial, I email the "contact us" page on that company's website and calmly tell them why I find their material offensive. It's a small thing, but it's amazing how loud an individual voice can be at times. If more folks would stand up against the trash on the Internet and in the media today, I think we could see change for good. Ephesians 5:11 says "Have nothing to do with the fruitless deeds of darkness, but rather, expose them," and it's time we do less accepting or ignoring, and do more exposing.

Technology and the Internet is an extremely important area that we as parents need to pay attention to if we want to parent well. There are many useful things associated with the amazing technologies of today, but there are many bad and hurtful things as well. A certain level of insidiousness also exists because our children can see and hide things with their phone that we as parents might never know about. Start a conversation with your children early in their lives about the issues and dangers of the Internet, do what you can to monitor things, and pray for God's protection over your children every single day.

TO CONSIDER:

1. How has technology helped your family? How has it hurt your family?

2. What can you do to protect your children from the bad side of modern technology?

3. Do you place limits on your children's online activities?

4. What are your thoughts on the Internet being a huge drug and gambling platform? Does this scare you as a parent?

5. What age is appropriate for kids to get their first phone, or if your kids have a phone, how old were they when they got it?

CHAPTER NINE

THE CROWDED TROPHY CASE AND NARCISSISM

"For all those who exalt themselves will be humbled,
and those who humble themselves will be exalted."
Luke 14:11

THAT'S FOR JUST SHOWING UP?

On my next birthday I will turn sixty. I am very fortunate to have both of my parents alive, and I go see them in Birmingham quite often. When I do, I spend the night in my growing-up bedroom. Talk about a time warp! Occasionally while I'm there I'll look at the trophies I won when I was a boy and remember the exact instance and feeling of winning each one. Some are for sports championships, and some are for making all-stars, but each one is special and represents a meaningful accomplishment of some sort.

Fast forward to when Madeline was in fifth grade in the very early 2000s. I coached her fifth grade basketball team, and we were out of our league (pun intended) and did not win a game all season. Most of the time we lost badly. After the particularly painful loss of the last game of the season, the team mom came up to me and asked if I was going to get the trophies or would I like her to handle it. I was not in the best of spirits because I don't like to lose, and I looked at her and said, "You must be kidding. We got our brains beat in all year and nobody gets a trophy for that." The team mom just assumed we would give the girls trophies because it was standard by that time to give everyone a trophy for having been on a team. That thought was foreign to me and did not make sense in my brain in any way. And that was my first taste of the "Everybody gets a Trophy" syndrome.

When I was a boy, parents probably swung the pendulum too far towards the "fend for yourself and just don't get killed and be home for dinner" philosophy. They had a "hope for the best" kind of attitude. In contrast, over the last couple of decades I've noticed the opposite begin to occur, with parents becoming involved in every minutia of their kids' lives and being terrified to let them feel any pain or sense of loss or failure. At times this includes the children being falsely rewarded for what is really just participation.

When you are in the adult world, you may get fired from your job. You may miss out on a promotion. You may get some really bad news regarding your health. If you have been shielded from and experienced little or no disappointment in the earlier part of your life, it will make it very difficult to navigate the setbacks that are sure to happen once you become a young adult. As a parent, if you allow your children to always feel like they've won, keep them from experiencing pain, and act like they just won the Super Bowl with everything they do, then you are stunting their growth towards being prepared for adulthood. You are also helping them have false confidence and perhaps an undue sense of pride.

REALLY REAL REALITY

Success is an awesome thing. Of course, you should celebrate your children's true successes and tell them often how proud you are of them. If they do something worthy, be the first to tell them and to affirm their accomplishment. However, when a failure occurs, don't sugarcoat or gloss over it. Let them realize they failed and help them work through it, and they will be much better people for it.

Part of what leads children to have a warped view of how the real world works is when parents over-inflate their achievements. It's a prime example of allowing good intentions to become bad parenting, and it gives the child a false sense of accomplishment that ultimately hurts more than it helps. Compliment them often, but don't act like they won the World Series every time they draw a picture or build a Lego house.

And there's a funny thing about your child's failures; they can present opportunities that help your child grow more than the victories do. In the failures, you can tell your children how proud you are by the way they handled the adversity, help them figure out the path to improve, and ultimately help them become more well-rounded, salt-of-the-earth people. This, of course, leads to them having a better sense of determination, resolve, and humility.

When I was in junior high school, they picked all-stars in our Junior Pro basketball league, and I made the team. All of us on the team thought we were really something, and we went into the qualifying rounds for the national tournament as a bunch of cocky basketball players. The games were only four quarters of eight minutes each, and in the first round we were beaten 122-14. Yes, 122-14. Needless to say, we all left the gym quite humbled. Later, several of the players on the opposing team did end up playing collegiate basketball and two of them actually played in the NBA, so that made me feel a little better down the road. In any case, I hate losing probably more than anyone I know, but experiencing that defeat was good because it was extremely humbling, and humility was something I was lacking in that situation. Developing traits such as humility is far more important than always winning. After all, objective self-realization is a beautiful thing.

WINNERS AND LOSERS

There really are winners and losers in life. There's no way around that fact, and great life lessons can be learned from both winning and losing. However, it seems that society today is doing its best to keep our kids from feeling a sense of pain or disappointment as long as possible. Some adults go out of their way to make sure no young people feel like they actually lost and that nobody feels too much like a winner either.

Here are some examples of things that have changed over the last several years to help young people avoid feelings of failure:

- Schools that have removed traditional grading or do not let anyone get a grade below a C because they don't want any student to feel they may not be as smart as another student

- Youth sports leagues that have done away with keeping score so no one feels like they lost

- Of course, the dreaded "participation awards," which de-emphasize the value of contribution and emphasize the importance of being recognized

- Schools that are removing the ability for students to be recognized as honor students so that no one else feels inferior

DIFFERENCES OF OPINION

There's another troubling phenomenon that has become front and center during the 2000's. More and more, society conditions people to only accept what they personally want to believe and not to give valid consideration to any other viewpoint. It's been sad over the last several years as intolerance has become the norm rather than a willingness to objectively listen to differing opinions. Of course, this is one of the factors that has led to many people placing an ever-increasing level of importance on "self." The unwillingness to listen to differing opinions is a similar situation to what Paul talks about in II Timothy 4:3 when he mentions people who have the desire to only hear "what their itching ears want to hear." He was talking about people who only believed what they wanted to believe and didn't listen or give any rational consideration to other beliefs. Here are some of the obvious ways this has manifested itself today:

- The creation of "cancel culture," where the expression of differing opinions is thought to be almost treasonous and calls for immediate retribution. When we teach or allow our children to be taught that they shouldn't consider or even listen to differing thoughts and ideas and should punish anyone with a different view or opinion, it creates a sense of narcissism and emotional weakness in them.

- University settings that produce a need for "safe spaces" for kids to work through the perceived emotional damage caused by someone disagreeing with them or from hearing a differing opinion in a lecture or campus speech. This is ultra-coddling and has helped make many of today's twenty-year-olds emotionally immature.

- The constant anger and vitriol hurled at people who express their opinion on social media. The resulting comments can often be flat-out mean and hateful, and that makes me wonder where civility has gone. It definitely doesn't seem to be on Facebook and other sites.

It's imperative that we teach our children that everyone is important and the opinions of other people matter, even if we don't agree with them. This is something that goes against the grain of today's thinking, but being hateful and acting ugly is never a good look on anyone. If your child always needs a safe space so he or she can deal with negative emotions, or if your children always feel like they are being wronged, or if everything is always someone else's fault, then you probably have some serious work to do as a parent.

MY CHILD, ENTITLED?

Without a doubt, there are definite indicators of individual entitlement. Some signs to look for are:

- Not being willing to help others
- Expecting to be always rescued from mistakes
- Always blaming other people or circumstances for failure
- Having a sense of materialism (whether it's getting a toy every time you go to the store or expecting the latest and greatest iPhone at midnight every time a new model comes out)
- Always trying to bargain to get their own way
- Thinking of themselves before anyone else
- Thinking the rules don't apply to them
- Being overly argumentative
- Having a lofty opinion of themselves

I believe it would be accurate to say that none of us want any of these attributes for our children.

KIDS, THEIR FRIENDS, AND STUFF

It is easy for parents to get caught up in the game of looking at what their children have and comparing it to what their friends' children have. When Madeline turned sixteen, we bought her a used Honda because I wasn't going to let her learn to drive with an expensive car. Also, we didn't think it would be a good idea to materialistically overdo it for her at that relatively young age. At the same time, I noticed the insane number of new BMWs and Lexus' in the school parking lot that many of her friends had received, and I was really surprised. Looking at that parking lot one day, I had a feeling that those kids were driving nicer cars than their parents. The parents seemed to not want their children to miss out on getting something their friend had, and it was almost like some sort of race to the top for the parents.

From my perspective, if a child gets a brand new $70,000 car when turning sixteen or is given the very best of everything while growing up, he or she is being taught that material things are more important than they really are. Materialism is one of the signs of an entitled child, and always being given the very best develops that sense in kids and makes it harder for their future spouses to be able to satisfy them materially. Leigh Ann told me about a time in a ladies' small group when a woman stood up and said, "Mothers, if you have a daughter, please stop setting our sons up for failure." She meant that if we give our daughters everything, it will make it more likely for their spouses to disappoint them later in life because the financial expectations will be too high going into the marriage.

It is important to let your kids hear the word "no" at times when it comes to material things. If you give them whatever they want every time they ask, then they will expect something all the time. With each time they get the next big thing, the impact and appreciation of the receiving diminishes. If you always give them the best of whatever it is that they are getting, then there's nowhere for them to go but down. As with everything in life, a healthy balance is best. Fight the temptation to give your children the biggest and best, even if you can afford it.

THE SPIRIT OF SERVANTHOOD

Have you noticed the feeling you get when you've gone out of your way and done something nice for someone, expecting nothing in return? It is amazing, and that is how God built us to be. Philippians 2:3 says, "Do nothing out of selfish ambition or vain conceit. Rather, in humility, value others above yourselves." Everything society teaches today goes against the concept of valuing others above ourselves, but in Matthew 5:14-16, Jesus says, "You are the light of the world…let your light shine before others, that they may see your good deeds and glorify your Father in heaven." One of the ways we let our light shine is our lives becoming more about other people and less about us. Loving and serving others should be a top priority, and we as parents should make every effort to have a servant's heart and to teach our children to do the same.

A focus on others will lead the entire family to have a much more fulfilling and rewarding life than one centered on self. Teaching children to have a servant's heart must start very early in life because, starting at a very young age, we all naturally lean towards being selfish. You can use little lessons about serving along the way that make a huge impact on who your children become as adults, but teaching the serving concept to them is a conscious decision you must make as a parent.

Our kids' growing-up house was in a nice neighborhood where everyone took pride in their yards and in the appearance of their homes. One day I drove by a particular house that looked ragged, with uncut grass and weeds.

It had been that way for quite a while, and I decided I was going to go home and write them a note and put it in their mailbox, chastising them for their lack of care and how they were making the entire neighborhood look. When I got home, Leigh Ann said she needed to borrow my truck. When I asked why, she said she was going to take her lawnmower and mow the yard of that exact house because she was worried that something might be wrong and they might have an illness or death in their family. After being run over with personal shame, I thought that was a great true-life illustration for a servant's heart. I am hopeful that we all (myself included) put away our pencils and get out our lawnmowers, and teach our kids to do the same.

HOW DO YOU TEACH YOUR CHILDREN TO HAVE SERVANT HEARTS?

Teaching our children to want to serve is not easy because it's not in us innately as humans to place others above ourselves. By the time children are one year old, they are already fighting with other kids in Mother's Day Out about who gets to play with a toy. Temper tantrums about not getting their way start early. But if you as a parent begin when they're young, you can teach your children to become more selfless, to have a heart that considers others before themselves, and to have a real heart of compassion towards the less fortunate. Reminds me of something called "the Golden Rule," where in Luke 6:31, Jesus said, "Do to others as you would have them do to you."

There is no better way to teach your children how to have a servant's heart than by example. If your children see you regularly going out of your way to be considerate of and to help others, I can promise it will give them food for thought, make them more aware of the service opportunities they personally have, and make it much more likely they will live a life of service. Leigh Ann has been much better than me about modeling this over our lives, and my kids took notice of her humble actions when it came to serving others.

Here are some examples to show your children what service looks like:

- Find regular service projects you can do as a family, such as serve days at church or monthly Saturdays providing meals to the less fortunate at a local shelter.

- Look for opportunities to be kind to people in situations that don't call for kindness. It might be as simple as putting change in a beggar's cup or leaving a larger tip than normal at a restaurant.

- Take time to have conversations with random people. There are a lot of people hurting very badly in the world right now, and a short conversation with your server, the person in line with you at the mall, or your mechanic could literally change the arc of their day (and life) in a positive way.

- Remind your children that it's important to befriend people at school who aren't the cool kids. We all remember kids in school who just didn't fit in and always seemed to have a tough time of it. There are still kids like that in every single school, and someone showing them just a little bit of kindness can drastically and positively change their perspective on life. Your child can be that person.

- Volunteer for service at church. Be an usher, fold programs, work in the nursery, or park cars.

- Take some of your extra stuff that you don't need and give it away, rather than letting it sit in your garage or basement or attic.

- Pay the bill for the car behind you when you're in a drive-through.

- Quietly let people know you are praying for them.

- Let someone go before you in a line.

- Pick up litter when you're out on a walk. It sounds like a strange thing, but it's an act of service that I've seen Leigh Ann do her entire life.

- Check in on somebody who doesn't expect you to check in on them. It's amazing the impact that can have on someone.

- Hold the door open for people.

- Make sure to give financially to places that need it.

- Go on a short-term mission trip as a family.

- Give compliments and words of encouragement frequently. My daughter-in-law Sloan is great about taking the time to hand-write meaningful notes, and as a recipient, I see firsthand how impactful those are.

Regularly talk to your children about the importance of serving others, and let them see how important it is to you by your actions. Serving is not a natural instinct, and it goes against the grain of the mindset in the USA today. But little by little, you can teach your children the spirit of service and servanthood.

———————

As a parent, you will have to overcome your instinct to make your kids always feel like they've won—or at least didn't lose—and I can promise that overcoming this instinct will take practice. Even when other parents are controlling every detail of their kids' lives and trying to make sure every step is as pain-free as possible, don't do the same with your children. Allow your kids to make mistakes and to experience failure, and then teach them about resilience and resolve. Let them know that people who have differing opinions are still to be respected. Finally, teach them about the humility and servanthood that Jesus was talking about in Matthew 19:30 when he said, "But many who are first will be last, and many who are last will be first." On the surface, all of this seems counter-intuitive to culture and to our own natural instincts, but in reality it leads to a much more fulfilling life of light.

TO CONSIDER:

1. What is unhealthy about rewarding your child when it is unwarranted?

2. Can you over-compliment your child?

3. What specific ways does society today ingrain a sense of entitlement in us and our children?

4. Do your children consistently blame someone else for their losses or shortcomings? If so, why?

5. What real life lessons can you use to teach your children to care more about others?

CHAPTER TEN

THE OIL OF THE EARTHLY LIFE ENGINE: MONEY

"But godliness with contentment is great gain, for we brought nothing into the world, and we can take nothing out of it." 1 Timothy 6:6-7

OIL THAT'S GREEN?

In many ways, money acts as the oil in the engine of earthly life. If oil gets dirty, or if it runs low, or if you pour it past full, the car engine can run rough or even grind to a halt in the middle of the interstate. Issues with the oil can make the other engine parts malfunction, even though on their own those parts are fine. The cylinder and pistons and valves may be okay, but if the oil is not right, the entire engine is affected.

Money acts the same way. If certain financial principles are not followed, household finances can malfunction, and family life begins to feel like an engine that is backfiring or won't even turn over.

DIRTY, EMPTY, AND LUMPY

When we think of financial problems, we tend to think that the only issue we can have with money is not having enough. Of course, if we never seem to have enough money, it can produce major issues in a family and in a marriage and will lead to some very stressful situations. Feeling broke all the time is never fun, and having to decide between paying the mortgage and paying the light bill can cause some uncomfortable feelings of self-defeat. Not having enough money is stressful, but there are other ways money can cause problems.

Think about the emphasis our culture places on "stuff." With the proliferation of social media over the last decade or so, exposure to new stuff and the corresponding pressure to have stuff has reached new heights. People can easily become fascinated by the latest and greatest and focus much of their energy on what they have or don't have. The trap of spending too much time thinking about the next thing we are going to buy or place we are going to visit is easy to fall into. The temptation to be, or at least appear, financially successful has never been stronger, and getting those likes on Instagram for fabulous vacation pics or the new Tesla seems to be very important to a whole lot of people.

I recently had a carpenter come to my house and make a very interesting comment. He said that he'd been in the business for a long time, and he's never seen as many people be "house poor" as he sees today. He said he does work at houses that are fancy on the outside but have lawn furniture on the inside because the homeowner couldn't afford anything else after spending every dime on the fancy house. Parents, there is no way around it—stuff never fully satisfies, and our character is way more important than our net worth. Having material things is nice, but it should be far down the list of important things in life.

Unexpected expenses are another area in which money can cause problems. Being frugal and planning for a rainy day is a lost art, and if we don't err on the side of being conservative when it comes to saving, it can come back to haunt us one day. Living paycheck to paycheck with no margin for error is stressful, and leading by example will help ingrain in our children that need for frugality and saving.

Money can tempt people to get into some harmful gray areas in terms of their integrity. Sometimes people can be honest in every other way but think it's okay to fudge a little on financial matters. For instance, the IRS is widely loathed; people hate paying taxes and will do whatever it takes to lessen their tax burden, even if it means getting into some gray areas or even flat-out cheating. Taking any deduction or "loophole" that the law allows is great, but cheating on your taxes is stealing. It's just like robbing a bank. Both are crimes in the law's eyes and in God's eyes, as there are no degrees of cheating. We are either honest or we are not. In Matthew 22:21, Jesus said, "...so give back to Caesar what is Caesar's and to God what is God's," which means that, like it or not, we have an obligation to pay what we owe in taxes. So, whether it's paying taxes, or receiving too much commission on a paycheck that nobody will find out about, or being given too much change at the gas station, God expects us to be 100 percent honest all the time in our finances and to teach our children to do the same.

TEACH THEM HOW TO CHANGE THE OIL

Money and finances are challenging and should be

included in how we prepare our children for the future. Surprisingly, this is one area that many parents don't think about as their kids are growing up, and then when the kids go to college or get married, they have no concept of basic financial knowledge. Since this is an area that can cause so much stress and so many problems later in life, it is critical that we as parents teach our children certain principles about money as they grow.

My four-year-old granddaughter Brooklyn has a piggy bank, and it has been interesting watching her start to learn about the concept of money. Of course, at four years old, it's hard for her to think about much more than getting some spare change from somebody to put in the piggy bank, but it's never too young to start teaching lessons about money to your kids.

As I mentioned earlier, we gave chores to Madeline and Max at an early age, and for completion of the chores, we gave them an allowance. Early on they learned about reward (allowance) for their labor (chores). As they grew older, there were certain things we would make them pay for so they could learn about expenses and make decisions about whether or not they really wanted to buy that thing or go to that concert. We provided for our kids, and they had a nice life growing up, but we didn't want to be a blank check for them. We made sure that they made some financial decisions on their own.

As our kids got older, we created special opportunities for them to be able to earn money. We would have projects that were over and above their chores where they could earn additional cash, and they would have to decide if they wanted to spend their time and effort to make money or not spend the time and not make money. Basically, the good ole "cost/benefit analysis" in action. Doing this helped Madeline and Max develop a strong work ethic that they both still have today, and it developed in them the sense that hard work leads to financial stability and opportunity.

When Madeline was getting married, I gave her a certain amount of money and told her she would pay for her wedding out of it (which was enough for a very nice wedding). If she had anything left over, she could use it to help buy her and Zac's first house. Boy, did their wheels start turning! They decided they would have a nice but smaller wedding and use a good bit of the money towards their first house. It was great watching them make some real-life decisions during that process—that is, until Madeline started marking some of my best friends off the guest list to save money! Needless to say, my close friends came to the wedding, but the overarching thought was that the entire process allowed them as a very young couple to make some major financial decisions, and that helped develop their future financial maturity.

I spent two years teaching finance at a college program at Church of the Highlands in Birmingham, AL., and it was very evident that many of those twenty-five college students didn't know much about applying finances to real life. How do you get a mortgage? What do you mean by "monthly bank reconciliation?" What is a credit score? What is an insurance deductible? I was glad to be able to teach my students the basics of various financial subjects, but that experience let me know that many of our college kids are going out into the world unprepared. Parents, I cannot overemphasize the fact that basic financial principles and knowledge is something that should be included in what you teach your children, because it will make their lives so much easier when they become adults.

Here are a few things you can do:

- Open a bank account for them when the time is right and let them see how that works.

- Get them a low-limit credit card to use, and then have them pay it each month from money you give them and/or money they earn.

- Teach them the importance of paying the credit card on time to avoid interest and to avoid late payments, which affects credit scores.

- If helping them develop a simple budget makes sense, then do it.

- Use some of the cool apps that are out there for young people to learn about and manage finances.

- Teach them early in their lives the magical concept of compounding interest.

- Put them in a position to make some financial decisions for themselves, even at an early age.

Overall, do your best to make sure they learn and become involved in some simple financial conversations and situations. Then it won't be such a shock when they start having to manage money and finances on their own.

SPENDING PRIORITIES

Spending priorities is a huge concept to instill in your children. While this goes against the world's standards, I believe giving money to help others should be on the top of the financial priority list.

If you're a Christian, giving begins with tithing, which is giving the first 10 percent of income to your church or a non-profit that does good in the community. This not only helps others, but it provides an internal satisfaction the way nothing else does. If times get tough, the natural response will be to cut back on the giving or tithing, but even when it seems like you won't make it financially if you tithe, I can promise that you will. In Luke 12:30-31, Jesus says, "For the pagan world runs after all such things, and your Father knows that you need them. But seek His kingdom, and these things will be given to you as well." God gives His absolute promise that if we seek His kingdom first, He will take care of us, and we can stand on that promise. Consistently teaching and modeling this to your children will lead them to have a spirit of giving.

At a very young age, before they had money of their own, we would give Madeline and Max a dollar bill each week to put in the offering bucket that came by every Sunday at church. You can bet there were times that their little eyes really wished they could keep that dollar, but they would still drop it in the bucket. That was a very early lesson that helped them see giving in action and to feel what it felt like to give.

There are always opportunities for giving that are over and above the tithe. Giving additional amounts of money can change lives, including the life of the giver. With so many people today unable to pay the electric bill, unable to put a full tank of gas in their car, or even being forced to decide between buying food or buying clothes, the opportunities for giving are everywhere. In Matthew 25:40, Jesus says, "...truly I tell you, whatever you did for one of the least of these brothers and sisters of mine, you did for me." He always was concerned about the less fortunate, and he wants us to be as well. Teaching your children to be givers first, even with their allowance money, will provide them with the valuable spiritual life lesson that if you give first, you are telling God that money is not and will not be your god and that you consider others more important than yourself.

Saving is the next priority after giving. Having cash saved up to weather a financial storm is critical, and it starts with teaching your children the importance of putting something away each month for that rainy day (which is sure to come). I owned a mortgage company for two decades and saw thousands of people's detailed financial situations, and it was amazing how many adults lived in $750,000 houses and drove nice cars but had zero runway if they had a financial setback. My client would have less than $1,000 in the bank and a $4,500 mortgage payment, two car payments of $700 each, and loads of credit card debt. One unexpected expense or the loss of a job and they were sunk, and that is a terrible way to live. Help your children early on to understand the importance of saving over spending.

After giving and saving comes living. Living means you can run your household with the money that's left and then pay for extras like vacations and eating out. Having a budget to plan out the basic, necessary living expenses is essential for being able to successfully navigate this. After paying for these basic expenses, you will know how much you have for the discretionary non-essentials. And if you don't have money for non-essentials after you give and save and pay for essentials, then you just don't have it. Consider other entertainment activities such as hikes, picnics, free concerts, and neighborhood get-togethers.

We as parents must model these spending priorities to our children in our own lives and actions. Be generous first, save for a rainy day, and then conservatively figure out where the rest of the money will go. If this is evident by your actions to your kids, they will take their own valuable life lesson from it.

LESS IS MORE

Maintaining financial margins means not always having the absolute top of the line things we can buy based on our income and accessibility of credit. If our kids see us spending like crazy over and above our means, then they will follow suit when they get older. Teach them that credit cards are not the way to finance life and not to ever allow themselves to get over-extended. Once that happens, it could take years to get out of it, and having stuff with the stress of the debt that goes with it is not worth it.

Social media has enabled people to post about their glorious and glamorous lives, but a lot of the time it's not their real lives—it's their online lives that they want you to believe. Then, as you look through the influencers or your friends' social feeds, the pressure to have more and more things starts, and this can lead to great discontentment. The pressure to look a certain way or have certain things is immense, and it is a trap that we have to guard against.

Parenting is a full-time job, and it's interesting how it graduates from teaching the kids to walk to teaching them to ride a bike to teaching them how to financially manage a household according to Biblical principles. I once heard someone say that you can tell everything you need to know about someone's life by looking through their checkbook ledger, and that really stuck with me. No matter what stage of life our children are in, the lessons they learn from us are important, and teaching them the financial lessons that they will use for the rest of their lives is a critical part of parenting well.

TO CONSIDER:

1. What are some experiences or situations where a family might have issues with money?

2. How important is it to teach your children the basic concepts of money? At what age should the teaching begin?

3. What are the priorities of your family when it comes to money and spending?

4. Do you think your children feel a lot of social pressure from comparing themselves to their friends and to social media influencers?

5. What have you specifically done to teach your children lessons about money and finances?

CHAPTER ELEVEN

THE HIERARCHY OF RELATIONSHIPS

"Hear, O Israel: The Lord our God, the Lord is one. Love the Lord your God with all your heart and with all your soul and with all your strength. These commandments that I give you today are to be on your hearts. Impress them on your children. Talk about them when you sit at home and when you walk along the road, when you lie down and when you get up. Tie them as symbols on your hands and bind them on your foreheads. Write them on the doorframes of your houses and on your gates."
Deuteronomy 6:4-9

MOM AND DAD

Isn't the "family dynamic" an interesting thing? It's almost like your family unit has a personality all its own,

SALT, LIGHT, & KIDS

comprised of how all the individual personalities of each member of the family interact together. Since your family itself has its own distinct personality, and you desire for the overall family personality to be as strong and vibrant as possible, then it makes sense to pay attention to all the individual interactions and relationships with each other. Simply put—how does each member of the family interact with the others, and how do you create a healthy family dynamic?

Over my many years of observing and mentoring families and leading family small groups, I have seen many instances where the parents have a stronger relationship with their kids than they do with each other. If that is the case, then the family is not functioning as God intended it. Moms and dads, your relationship with each other should take a higher priority than your relationship with your kids, and a healthy relationship between the parents that is clearly evident to the children does more for the children than probably any other influence in their life. If the mom and dad thing isn't working, the kids will notice, and it can significantly and adversely affect them.

If children think that Mom and Dad don't like each other or don't really care about each other, they might find themselves in the same situation with their future spouse, as a syndrome of weak marriages can generationally perpetuate itself. If a daughter knows that Mom cares more about her than Mom does for Dad, then the daughter will quickly figure out how to use that to her advantage. The children must see, as much as possible, that their parents love each other, care about each other, and place each other at a higher priority than they do the children. Parents should love their kids deeply and unconditionally, but the children should never feel that they are more important to their parents than Mom and Dad are to each other. Working hard on your relationship as spouses is a big part of parenting well, because if the spousal relationship isn't working, ultimately the parent/child relationship isn't going to work as well as it should.

In our house, the kids always knew that Mom came first for me, and vice-versa. Leigh Ann and I made sure our children knew that we loved each other. We always showed affection for each other in front of the kids, and we always treated each other with respect in front of them—and they took notice. It was not a good day for the kids if one of them disrespected Leigh Ann. My kids knew I loved them like crazy, but they also knew that Mom came first. To this day, both Madeline and Max and their spouses are proud of the relationship that Leigh Ann and I have, and to them it models a real, living example that marriages can work and work well.

Now, I'd be lying if I said marriage is easy. It is not, and marriages require the same level (if not more) of "leaving it all on the field" as parenting does. Leigh Ann and I had issues to work through over the years, but we always made sure we worked through them, and all those trials and the major effort we put in have led to our marriage being better now after thirty-five years than it ever has been before. My marriage is my biggest earthly blessing, but even in the best of times, our marriage takes a lot of work. Letting your kids see you consistently working hard at your marriage gives them great insight as to how their future marriages can be successful.

How do you get and maintain a strong marriage that you can model to your children? Of course, it would take an entire book (or two or three) to talk through that, but my focus here is to make sure you place a very high importance on working on your marriage, both for the sake of the marriage and for the sake of your sons and daughters. Go on weekly date nights, spend casual time together just hanging out, treat each other with great respect, and pray every day for God to help your marriage. Of course, if you are a single parent, you are presented with unique challenges, but you can still model healthy adult relationships for your kids with co-workers, friends, and people you might be dating. Your children are watching you all the time, and being able to see what healthy adult relationships look like will do wonders in guiding their own relationships as they grow older.

PARENTING AS ONE

How do you parent well together as a father-and-mother unit? As I mentioned earlier, it is important for the kids to know that the relationship between their parents is the most important relationship among the family members, and we as parents must hold each other accountable for being good parents. There were many times over the years that Leigh Ann would encourage me to act differently in speaking to or punishing our kids. She had more of an inside track on their minds and thinking in particular situations. She was with them more than I was because I was at work. If she felt there was a better way for me to handle a particular situation, she would tell me so. Then it was up to me to have enough humility to think about it and realize she was probably right. There also were times that she would want to overlook something that I felt strongly about not overlooking, and I would tell her why we needed to deal with a situation a certain way. There was back and forth in all these situations, but our mutual thoughts and discussions would lead to the best answer much more frequently than if we made parenting decisions on our own. The parental accountability we had was nice because our decisions together were more solid than our individual decisions would have been. After all, iron does sharpen iron.

THE UNIFIED FRONT

What do you do if you and your spouse are at an impasse on a particular situation or decision? As unpopular as it may be, I still go back to the Biblical answer. Colossians 3:18-19 says, "Wives, submit yourselves to your husbands, as is fitting in the Lord. Husbands, love your wives and do not be harsh with them." What that verse teaches is that, ultimately, the father should make the final decision, but along with that comes treating his wife with love and respect.

Once you make a decision about your kids, make sure to present a unified front to them, even if one of you might not totally agree with the decision. The kids will try to play you against each other, but it's critical that they know that you as parents are a team and that you stand by each other. You are going to disagree with your spouse at times, and your kids watching you successfully navigate conflict resolution is great.

Please do not yell and scream at each other in front of the kids—or ever, for that matter—because yelling and screaming never accomplish anything good. I have people very close to me who grew up in a house of constant yelling and screaming, and the long-term negative effects on the children living in that environment are traumatic. Occasionally raising your voice a bit is fine, but anything beyond a raised voice to your kids or spouse is not cool. Constantly being angry and yelling undermines the very fabric our relationships are built on and leads to unstable feelings by the kids towards you as parents. It can also lead to a very unhealthy marriage, which might ultimately lead to divorce. If your house is on fire, it's okay to yell. Otherwise, it's not.

Moms, it is a fact that you usually control the general mood in the house more than anyone. If you are consistent and positive and happy most of the time, it will bleed over into your children and husband. I know it can be challenging and is probably not a duty that most moms relish, but moms are the glue of the family in a lot of ways. You moms can impact the family dynamic in a positive way more than anyone else!

DIVORCE

These days, divorce is very commonplace, and many people feel like it's the best solution for their problems. There is no doubt that divorce at times can be tough to avoid, but it sure can come with some unhealthy consequences for children. If you are married, I'd like to encourage you to try hard not to even have the word divorce be part of your family vocabulary, and not to have it be an option. Try going to counselors, reading books on healthy marriages, praying for healing in your marriage—doing whatever it takes to avoid divorce. The Bible gives one exception for allowable divorce—marital unfaithfulness—and that is a good rule to live by.

Of course, almost as important as avoiding divorce is being civil and treating each other with respect, even if you don't like each other all the time. If kids see a continuously dysfunctional relationship between Mom and Dad, that can be almost as bad as divorce. I love James 1:19, which says, "…Everyone should be quick to listen, slow to speak and slow to become angry." Remembering those words will help nurture a successful marriage relationship.

OTHER FAMILY MEMBERS

Several people close to me have extended family members who create a lot of dysfunction in their immediate family unit. As parents, you should do everything you can to make sure relationships with other close family members are as strong, or at least as non-abrasive, as possible. Romans 12:18 says, "If it is possible, as far as it depends on you, live at peace with everyone." Do everything you can for all relationships to be at least civil, and if those certain extended family relationships are irreparable, bite your tongue and move on. Refuse to continue to engage in an ongoing argument with extended family members that will fester and do damage to your own family unit. Our children will take cues from us as to how adults should treat other adults, and that includes how we treat our extended family members.

THE APEX OF THE TRIANGLE

While the relationship between parents is important for the family to work properly, I contend that a household that doesn't place God firmly at the top and front and center is missing the most important piece of the relationship hierarchy.

When it comes to parenting, God, Jesus, and the Holy Spirit can provide guidance like no website, blog, or friend's advice. Through scripture, prayer, and promptings of the Holy Spirit, you can be fully led through the proverbial parenting desert. Placing God first helps you as a person to become who He intends—someone who is loving, patient, thoughtful, wise, and kind. If God isn't in charge and we are left to our own devices, it is easy to step off the path that we need to be on for both our spouse and for our children.

As I mentioned earlier, we had some parenting challenges with my son Max as he grew older into his teen years. At times it was frustrating, but I'll tell you what made it easier. In Proverbs 22:6, the Bible says, "Train up a child in the way he should go, and when he is old, he will not depart from it." We hung on the promise of that verse many, many times when we were in the middle of those challenges. Thankfully, a promise from God is exactly that—a promise—and today Max is a close follower of Jesus. We worked hard to train him up in the way he should go, and that verse made us feel (relatively) confident during those years when it was not easy to see a positive outcome. His sister also has a great relationship with God, and so do their spouses Zac and Sloan. There is no question the strong relationship they all have with Jesus is by far the most satisfying part of being Madeline and Max's parents.

During some of the challenging times we had in Madeline's journey as a teenager, we would always pray for God to reveal things to us so we could make the decisions we needed to make. It was amazing how faithful He was in those situations and in answering those prayers by putting people in our paths and things in our lives that let us know exactly what we needed to know or do. Our own human intellect just wasn't enough.

BEING A LIVING EXAMPLE OF FAITH

If you are a Christian, please do everything you can to live your faith loudly and consistently in front of your kids. This is what Jesus meant when he talked about being the salt of the earth and the light of the world. If you profess to be a Christian but live another way, they will quickly be turned off from the whole prospect of Christianity. Gen Z (born between 1995-2010) and Generation Alpha (born after 2010) are looking for meaning and faith in something, have a general suspicion of Christianity, and are leaving the Christian faith at a faster pace than any generation before. To many of them, Christianity is a Republican thing, a Southern thing, or even an anti-masking thing. If you are a Christian but are not authentic, it's going to be easy and natural for your children to look for faith and meaning somewhere else. And that's likely what a lot of their friends could be doing.

Here are some things you can do to encourage your children in their Christian faith:

- Talk about spiritual things in a non-judgmental way as a family.

- Say a prayer before every meal and before they go to bed.

- Use any opportunity to show your children how a certain scripture came to life in your lives.

- Have a simple but regular family devotional.

- Go to church regularly as a family.

- Let them see your faith in action by serving and helping others.

- Encourage them to be a part of the youth group at church.

- Finally, be sure they see you treating people the way God expects us to treat them. If you are genuine and sincere, they will respond positively.

And here's the most critical statement I will make in this entire book: **I fully believe that the most important part of your job as a parent is helping to instill faith in Christ in your children so that they have eternal life in Heaven.** No decision they make will come anywhere close to being as important as that one.

CHURCH ATTENDANCE

Church attendance overall is the lowest it's ever been in the United States. In 2020, a Gallup poll found that for the first time in their eighty-year analysis, less than half of Americans belonged to a church, synagogue, or mosque[6]. At the turn of the century, the number was 70 percent, so the decline in religious attendance has been precipitous. It's not that surprising, though, because fewer and fewer people are expressing a faith in God and Jesus. Between loads of other available activities, busyness during the week that makes everyone want to rest on the weekends, and an increasing apathy, church attendance has been hit hard. However, consistently going to church as a family shows honor to God and puts you and your children in a position to have good Christian friends and be surrounded by like-minded people. With all the distractions of today, consistently going to church will take a sincere commitment from you as a family. You just have to decide to do it, and then do it.

When I was growing up, my parents took me to church every single week until I left home for good. I also was really involved in the church youth group (that's where I met Leigh Ann), and those were some of the best times of my life. I had friends outside of church, but my core base of friends was always from church, and that was because I regularly attended and

---

6   "U.S. Church Membership Falls Below Majority for First Time." News. Gallup.Com. Gallup, March 29, 2021. /https://news.gallup.com/poll/341963/church-membership-falls-below-majority-first-time.aspx.

was able to make those deep friendship connections that I still have to this day.

With the Internet and streaming and with youth sports playing on Sundays (that never was the case when I was growing up), it's easy not to attend church at all or get out of the habit of attending. Your family dynamic will reap great rewards if you make sure to regularly attend church, and it will also increase the chances that your children will be able to develop some strong friendships with people who are positive influences on them.

PRAYER IN PARENTING

I don't think anything in parenting is as important as prayer. Prayer can move mountains, give you parental insights that you would not have on your own, and lets God know how important your children are to you. Leigh Ann and I always had a written prayer list going for our kids, and we made sure to faithfully pray every day for them. We still do to this day. Some things you can pray for are a daily blessing over them, protection from harm, for their friends, and for specific challenges and situations they have at a particular time in their life. Pray for them to have a heart chasing after God, for their future spouses, and for their health. Be consistent in praying for them, because as James 5:16 says, "...the prayer of a righteous person is powerful and effective." Sometimes prayer is all you have when it comes to parenting.

WHEN DOES THE TRAINING START?

It's never too early to start training them up in the way they should go spiritually. Satan has masterfully taken over society at an ever-increasing rate and has figured out ways to get himself ingrained with our kids at a younger and younger age. Things that used to be widely held as unacceptable and that went against the Word of God are now widely accepted and even embraced by our society. Just scroll through the movie choices on Netflix sometime and see the high percentage that are rated R. The media intake of this young generation is overwhelming and at times damaging to them, and they don't even realize it. The sinful things they have at their fingertips are very scary.

Again, we as parents must model purity for them. I remember the exact moment in 1995 when Leigh Ann and I decided we would never watch another R-rated movie, and it was a watershed moment for us. If your kids see you watching junk on TV, then they are going to do the same. The intake of unwholesome and unholy stuff cannot help but make a person be more unwholesome and unholy. It's very easy to rationalize that a movie full of violence or nudity doesn't affect you, but it does. Be a model for your children and get that kind of thing out of your life. Don't be afraid to refuse to let your children watch certain things, even though their friend next door gets to. Peer pressure on them can also be peer pressure on you as a parent, and it's up to you to stand against it.

US AGAINST THE WORLD

The forces of today's culture are immense. Modern culture says if you're living your best life and satisfying your own personal desires, then everything's great. Nothing could be further from the truth. The words of the Bible are immutable, and much of society today totally disregards those Biblical teachings on almost every issue.

As parents, make sure to teach your children that it's okay to go against today's societal grain and to stand up for things the Bible teaches. Teach them that it's good for them to stand up for morality and principles, even if they are on the receiving end of some negativity. Teach them that it's okay not to endorse lifestyles and not to be silent about beliefs that are incongruent with God. More than ever, true Christians today are scoffed at and rejected, and if that happens to you and your family, wear it as a badge of honor. And of course, love everybody no matter what.

God first, Mom and Dad second, kids third. If you decide on the front end of parenting that those are going to be your family's relationship priorities, and if you work hard to make that the hierarchy of relationships in your family, you will reap great rewards. Your family dynamic will thrive, be at its absolute best, and work just as God intended.

TO CONSIDER:

1. What role, if any, does God play in your family?

2. Do you ever find yourself favoring your children over your spouse? Do you think this is harmful to the family dynamic?

3. What are some specific things moms and dads should do when it comes to parenting together?

4. In what ways can you model a strong marriage for your children?

5. What does the promise of Proverbs 22:6 mean to you?

CHAPTER TWELVE

LEAVING IT ALL ON THE FIELD

"Whatever you do, work at it with all your heart,
as working for the Lord, not for human masters."
Colossians 3:23

In 2000, one particular quarterback was unceremoniously drafted during the sixth round of the NFL draft. Six other quarterbacks were drafted before him, and expectations for him were low. He got a break, was put in the starting lineup, and was given a shot that started him on his way to becoming the greatest quarterback (and possibly the greatest football player) of all time. Of course, I'm talking about Tom Brady.

How did Tom succeed? Out of college it was not apparent that he had amazing gifts. That's why 198 other players were selected before him during that year's draft.

What Tom Brady had was an insatiable desire to succeed and a work ethic that was (and is to this day) second to none. He watched more game film than everybody else, paid more attention to his diet than everybody else, worked out more than everybody else, threw more footballs than everybody else, and day in and day out he just outworked everybody. And he is now the GOAT.

As parents, we need to have the same work ethic as Tom Brady when it comes to leading our kids. It can be said that Tom is a guy who leaves it all on the field every day, meaning he consistently does everything possible he can do in order to get better, to excel, and to win the game. We may not be the best parent ever, but if we leave it all on the field in parenting every day, we can and will be the absolute best parent we can be. Everyone has certain limitations, but there is no limitation to the amount of work, care, and desire we can have to be a great parent.

"Work at it with all your heart." This phrase applies to every aspect of life and encourages us to give a full and complete effort with everything we do. Whether it's performing what we feel are menial tasks at our jobs, leading a small group, lining the field before one of our kid's games, or having parking lot duty at church, God expects us to do everything with excellence. And this definitely applies to parenting.

For most people it's easy to become a parent, but it is difficult to parent well. Working at it as hard as you possibly can is the only way to truly parent well. That doesn't mean just doing more stuff for your kids; it means pouring your time, thought, and energy into how to parent the best way possible, and then executing it. It means leaving it all on the field.

Leaving it all on the field means thinking less about what would benefit your individual life and thinking more about what would benefit your kids in ways that help them grow, and learn, and mature. There will be times where you are tired, when you don't want another confrontation with your kids, or when you don't want to have to take them somewhere again on a Friday night. Parenting well will require those things, and we as parents need to be willing to spend the time and energy it takes, even when we don't feel like it. I remember when Madeline's entire fifth grade took a trip to Washington, D.C., and Leigh Ann did not want to go at all. She tried to figure out a way out of it because she was not a fan of hotels and twenty-hour bus rides, but after a while she gave in and went as a chaperone. They ended up having an amazing time together, and it was one of the highlights of Madeline's grade school years. They still have stories from that trip that they talk about, and if Leigh Ann had not gone the extra parenting mile, they would be robbed of one of the highlights of Madeline's childhood.

Leaving it all on the field means having enough humility to recognize when you're wrong and being able to admit it, and then changing your course of action. Both of my kids were in a private Christian school into their junior high school years, and I had no doubt they would finish high school there. At the end of the summer after her eighth grade year, Madeline came to us and said she wanted to go to the local public high school. Being a person who speaks before thinking sometimes, I immediately gave a resounding, "No," and that was the end of the discussion. That is, until Leigh Ann came to me and said we should see what God's will was before I shut the discussion down (Leigh Ann has always been and still is in many ways my "voice of reason"). I didn't even want to consider it, but I begrudgingly told Madeline to write down a list of reasons why we should allow her to go to the public high school. In about an hour, we had a detailed list from her with probably fifteen reasons she should change schools, and they all made total sense. I immediately knew that she should go to the public high school, and in two days she was there for the start of her freshman year. It was absolutely the best decision for her and was a clear example that, in my flesh, I didn't always know best. Funny enough, we had the exact same thing happen with Max the next year. I am very glad God removed my obstinate nature in both of those situations.

Leaving it all on the field does not mean we should push ourselves and our kids to exhaustion with activities and allow them to dominate all our time. Parenting well many times will require an inaction or just saying no, rather than an action and a "yes" answer, even when the "no" answer is not the easiest answer to give. But as much as possible, our decisions should be made based on what's best for our children, and at times those decisions will call for less activity and maybe some disappointed kids.

Leaving it all on the field means working hard to always have open and honest lines of communication with your children. There's really nothing more effective in parenting than developing a relationship with your children early on that allows both you and them to talk freely about uncomfortable subjects. This will become more and more important (and more and more difficult) the older they get.

Leaving it all on the field means doing everything you can at a healthy level when it comes to loving and affirming your kids. Tell them often that you are proud of them and make them feel affirmed and confident as human beings. Make sure you tell them you love them often and that they know you care deeply for them, want the best for them, and think they're pretty awesome. Just avoid taking this too far and telling them all the time that they are the greatest thing ever and that everything they do is magical. That only leads to a false sense of pride and a lack of humility and will probably lead to some uncomfortable proverbial smacks in the face for them later in life.

Leaving it all on the field means teaching our children what it means to truly become and consistently be a responsible person. Our instinct as parents is to make their lives as easy as possible, but allowing them (and ourselves) to be in situations that may not be the easiest teaches them life skills and how to be a responsible person. This will require more effort on our part as parents, but over the course of their lives, our children will benefit greatly from having been put in positions, even at an early age, that require them to assume responsibility, perform tasks, and make their own decisions. These days, a young person who has a broad array of life skills is a bit difficult to find, and that is because my own generation of parents became the first ones who started trying to do everything for their kids and to protect them from every bad thing. It's time for you younger parents to reverse this trend.

Leaving it all on the field will unfortunately require you at times to let your children suffer consequences. This is not an easy part of parenting, but letting them navigate difficult situations and not always coming to their rescue will help them develop emotional soundness and maturity much more quickly and will benefit them greatly as they grow into adults.

Leaving it all on the field requires you to put a lot of thought and prayer into how and when to punish. Keeping a delicate balance with punishing is a constant you will have to deal with, starting even as young as one year old. Punishing is never fun for them or for you, and a great deal of wisdom is needed in what can be a regular occurrence.

Leaving it all on the field requires you to invest time in getting to know your children's friends and even their parents. Their friends can ultimately have more influence than anyone else, including you, and it will pay off greatly for you to do your best to arrange situations and life so you have opportunities to have relationships with their biggest influences.

Leaving it all on the field will require you to be involved at some level with who they date. Their boyfriends and girlfriends will have more influence on them than anybody else. Even if it's uncomfortable or unwanted at times, make sure you really know their boyfriends and girlfriends. Who they marry will be their biggest earthly decision, and your wisdom and instinct can play a big part in helping them make sure they don't make a big mistake.

Leaving it all on the field means teaching your kids how to be pure-minded and pure-hearted as the Bible calls for us all to be. Teach them how to be pure with their bodies and minds, and do this by word and example. Take an inventory of what your family is consuming when it comes to technology, social media, TV, and movies, and then make the necessary changes so you can clear the pathway for your kids to have pure minds and hearts.

Leaving it all on the field may require you to change some things you are personally doing. Parents, if you are watching shows and streaming series and movies that are not pure, your kids will take note and fill their young and impressionable minds with the same kind of stuff. People today have been fooled by Satan into thinking that it's okay to put trash in their minds, and many have become insensitive to the fact that what they are watching or consuming is disappointing to God. Filthy language, extreme violence, and gratuitous sex are trash in God's eyes and should be in our eyes as well. Decide to stop, and then have a family conversation about why you stopped. If your children see that a pure mind is important to you, it is much more likely that having a pure mind will be important to them. If you are behaving poorly and divisively on social media as a parent, make an effort to stop those derisive and divisive comments and posts, and then tell your kids why you have decided to stop. Our actions speak louder than a million words, and letting your kids know that you aren't perfect and want to make some changes for the better is okay. Actually, it's great. They will see that Mom and Dad are interested in being better people and that desire will carry over into their own lives.

Leaving it all on the field means teaching your children how to be good, decent, kind, salt-of-the-earth humans. It means teaching your children to be honest, even with little things, to be trustworthy and loyal friends who don't backstab or talk about other people behind their backs, to have a servant's heart that is happy to cut the grass of the elderly lady down the street—and to do it for free. It means teaching them to give adults the respect they deserve and have earned by living a long life, and to respect teachers, coaches, principals, pastors, and anyone in a position of authority. Our society today has de-emphasized respecting others and it is time for mutual respect to be brought back, even for people who might disagree with us on politics, or sports, or religion.

Leaving it all on the field means teaching your children not to let the culture of the day determine how they act and what they believe. The Bible should be the ruling authority in our lives, not what some talking head on TV or some tech giant CEO or some politician or some teacher at school tells you and your kids. Don't be afraid to stand up against things that modern society espouses that clearly go against what God tells us. Love everybody through patience and kindness, but don't mistake love with accepting lifestyles that are against what God teaches us, even if people tell you that you are hateful or insensitive. Filter everything through what God says in the Bible, not through what society says. And remember that a clear conscience doesn't mean you are innocent in your actions. Only abiding by what the Word says makes you innocent.

Leaving it all on the field means teaching your children that they can and should influence their friends for good. It's amazing how people are drawn to the light of good people just like a moth is drawn to a flame. Teach your children they really can be the light of the world in a place that is dark in so many ways, and to let their light shine through their humility and kindness to others.

Finally, leaving it all on the field means teaching your children about God's place in their hearts and lives. Our time on earth is just a blink of an eye, and our time in eternity will be forever. There is nothing you can do that is as important as teaching your children to have an eternal perspective. Jesus died on the cross for our sins and gives us a chance through grace to accept Him so that we may live with Him and His Father forever. There is no decision your child (and you) will ever make that comes close to being as important as what you and your family will decide to do with Jesus.

Amen. Come, Lord Jesus.

TO CONSIDER:

1. How important is it and how difficult is it to give maximum effort when it comes to parenting?

2. Do you find yourself ever taking shortcuts in parenting? In what ways?

3. How difficult in today's culture is it to teach your children how to go against culture and be pure-minded, and what steps do you take to focus on this very important part of parenting?

4. How important is it to parent by example rather than just by word?

5. What to you is the most important goal in parenting?

AFTERWORD

FROM STEVE'S SON, MAX:

My relationship with my parents is something I will be forever grateful for. Go ahead and take this as my stamp of approval and a real-life experience five-star review for my mom and dad.

One thing to note is that it was not a straight and linear path to the point we are today. Great relationships take time, space, nurturing, communication, and, in my own experience of being a Hines, God. While I can't expect everyone reading this to be a Christian (and that's ok—this entire book will still be applicable), there are values all throughout the Bible that I saw practiced by both of my parents, and those values ultimately made them better parents to me and my sister. My parents had a great understanding that they needed to be my parents way more than they needed to be my friends as I grew up, and now that I am twenty-eight, they have become two of my closest friends. Thankfully, there are still times in my life where I ask them questions as a parent and not just a friend.

My parents spent a lot of time with Madeline and me as we grew up, and that was crucial for our healthy upbringing. My mom was an A+ stay-at-home-mom, is the most servant-hearted person I know, and poured into our lives every single day. My dad was the monetary "mule" of the family, providing income and resources so my mom could raise us at home. One noteworthy aspect of this dynamic is my dad worked a lot but still made sure to commit time to the family, and a lot of it. He understood that not working an extra hour and making sure he was home for dinner was a net positive, even if that meant his business ventures were "one hour behind." Fathers need to be present in the home, and that has sadly disappeared in a lot of today's family structures. My dad also coached and practiced with me at home for a lot of my sports life (good thing he was the one who broke the window with a lacrosse ball and not me!), and my mom always was the hero at halftime with bags of fruit and peanut bars.

Growing up, I knew that both of my parents cared a lot, but they let me have enough space to figure out certain things myself, and they also let me get in trouble—but not without consequences. They also were very supportive of anything I wanted to pursue, whether that be a new sport, purchasing a musical instrument, or changing colleges. They supported me giving up a full academic scholarship at the University of Alabama and transferring to Belmont University in Nashville to pursue the music business, and that was a decision that totally changed my life in so many positive ways, including finding my amazing wife Sloan.

I didn't fully realize it growing up, but I am very fortunate to have my parents. I didn't agree with their decisions all the time for sure and we butted heads often, but looking back now I see how certain decisions they made turned out to be the best for me. I can honestly say that I owe a lot of who I've turned out to be as a man to my mom and dad and the way they parented me over the years.

FROM STEVE'S DAUGHTER, MADELINE:

While sitting outside on this beautiful Fall day during my littlest baby's nap time, and doing my best to put this together with my newly self-diagnosed ADHD (Ha!) and a great side order of "mom brain", here goes! In a nutshell (cashews being a personal fav), my childhood was happy and simple. I knew I was loved, and I knew my parents loved each other (forever beating that 50 percent!). My brother and I were greatly provided for, and we grew up surrounded by many friends and family. Now that I'm a parent myself (to the two best girls in the entire world!) I see how important it is to keep things fun—I adore me some fun—all the while trying to help your children become the best people they can, and that was the case in our home growing up. Both of my parents also worked hard to set a Godly foundation and family structure that gave us great stability and many amazing childhood memories. Today, my parents are always available with their time and energy for my girls, and that has also made my parenting journey quite a bit easier! All of this to say, I love and appreciate my parents greatly!

FROM STEVE'S DAUGHTER-IN-LAW, SLOAN HINES:

Mr. Steve is my father-in-law, my husband Max's father. From the very beginning of Max and I dating, Mr. Steve would always make a very intentional point to get to know me. I remember he would randomly send me a text to ask how I was doing or send me photos of Max when he was little. He even decided to have a thoughtful nickname for me and calls me by my middle name—Frances! All these little things he did early in our relationship certainly did not go unnoticed and made me feel welcomed and a part of the family from the very beginning. I am so grateful to have such a great father-in-law like Mr. Steve.

His dedication to his children and grandchildren even caused him and Mrs. Leigh Ann to move from Birmingham to Nashville to be with all of us. Since they have lived in Nashville, we have built a closer relationship because of the effort that he and Mrs. Leigh Ann put into our family. At least once a week, Mr. Steve and Mrs. Leigh Ann have us over for dinner and we have intentional quality time together. If we don't meet at their welcoming home, we meet for food, go to movies, or go to fun events in the city. Not to mention, they always pay for everyone so generously and graciously.

Being a part of a family that is healthy, loves each other, and genuinely has a good relationship is such a blessing and something I will never take for granted. It almost brings me to tears when I think about all the little things Mr. Steve and Mrs. Leigh Ann did to make me feel part of "the gang." Whether it is inviting me on family vacations, sitting together at church, giving little gifts, or giving hugs and words of affirmation, they always make me feel so welcomed and loved.

When the family is together, Mr. Steve demonstrates such humility and faith to the Lord by praying before every meal and thanking God for everything we are blessed with. He truly is an undeniable servant to the Lord and spiritual leader of the household. I can always count on him for a deep spiritual talk about the Bible, Jesus, and the Holy Spirit. Thankfully, my husband Max took after his father in this aspect.

Max shared with me about how his dad took the time to coach his lacrosse, basketball, and baseball teams growing up. He also spent countless hours throwing football and shooting basketball with Max, and Max definitely gets his competitiveness from his dad as well as his love for Alabama football (of course!). It's an admirable thing that Mr. Steve was able to build a successful business and provide for his family while also being fully present in his children's lives. Max is a phenomenal man because of his parents and thanks to Jesus! It's because of his parents' faith that Max has such a strong foundation built on the Lord. To know Mr. Steve is a joy and I am beyond grateful to be his daughter-in-law.

ACKNOWLEDGMENTS

First of all, I'd like to thank God, Jesus, and the Holy Spirit, through whom this book was born and through whom all things are possible. I'd like to thank Leigh Ann, who has been by my side for every step of our 30+ year parenting journey. Thanks to my children, Madeline and Max, for the joy they bring and for their wonderful friendship. Also, thanks to their spouses, Zac and Sloan, for becoming and being such a huge part of our family.